WORLD BANK TECHNICAL PAPER NUMBER 179
AFRICA TECHNICAL DEPARTMENT SERIES

Indigenous Integrated Farming Systems in the Sahel

The World Bank
Washington, D.C.

AFRICA TECHNICAL DEPARTMENT SERIES

Technical Paper Series

No. 122 Dessing, *Support for Microenterprises: Lessons for Sub-Saharan Africa*

No. 130 Kiss, editor, *Living with Wildlife: Wildlife Resource Management with Local Participation in Africa*

No. 132 Murphy, Casley, and Curry, *Farmers' Estimations as a Source of Production Data: Methodological Guidelines for Cereals in Africa*

No. 135 Walshe, Grindle, Nell, and Bachmann, *Dairy Development in Sub-Saharan Africa: A Study of Issues and Options*

No. 141 Riverson, Gaviria, and Thriscutt, *Rural Roads in Sub-Saharan Africa: Lessons from World Bank Experience*

No. 142 Kiss and Meerman, *Integrated Pest Management and African Agriculture*

No. 143 Grut, Gray, and Egli, *Forest Pricing and Concession Policies: Managing the High Forests of West and Central Africa*

No. 157 Critchley, Reij, and Seznec, *Water Harvesting for Plant Production*, vol. II: *Case Studies and Conclusions for Sub-Saharan Africa*

No. 161 Riverson and Carapetis, *Intermediate Means of Transport in Sub-Saharan Africa: Its Potential for Improving Rural Travel and Transport*

No. 165 Kellaghan and Greaney, *Using Examinations to Improve Education: A Study in Fourteen African Countries*

Discussion Paper Series

No. 82 Psacharopoulos, *Why Educational Policies Can Fail: An Overview of Selected African Experiences*

No. 83 Craig, *Comparative African Experiences in Implementing Educational Policies*

No. 84 Kiros, *Implementing Educational Policies in Ethiopia*

No. 85 Eshiwani, *Implementing Educational Policies in Kenya*

No. 86 Galabawa, *Implementing Educational Policies in Tanzania*

No. 87 Thelejani, *Implementing Educational Policies in Lesotho*

No. 88 Magalula, *Implementing Educational Policies in Swaziland*

No. 89 Odaet, *Implementing Educational Policies in Uganda*

No. 90 Achola, *Implementing Educational Policies in Zambia*

No. 91 Maravanyika, *Implementing Educational Policies in Zimbabwe*

No. 101 Russell, Jacobsen, and Stanley, *International Migration and Development in Sub-Saharan Africa*, vol. I: *Overview*

No. 102 Russell, Jacobsen, and Stanley, *International Migration and Development in Sub-Saharan Africa*, vol. II: *Country Analyses*

No. 132 Fuller and Habte, editors, *Adjusting Educational Policies: Conserving Resources while Raising School Quality*

No. 147 Jaeger, *The Effects of Economic Policies on African Agriculture: From Past Harm to Future Hope*

Manufactured in the United States of America
First printing August 1992

Technical Papers are published to communicate the results of the Bank's work to the development community with the least possible delay. The typescript of this paper therefore has not been prepared in accordance with the procedures appropriate to formal printed texts, and the World Bank accepts no responsibility for errors.

The findings, interpretations, and conclusions expressed in this paper are entirely those of the author(s) and should not be attributed in any manner to the World Bank, to its affiliated organizations, or to members of its Board of Executive Directors or the countries they represent. The World Bank does not guarantee the accuracy of the data included in this publication and accepts no responsibility whatsoever for any consequence of their use. Any maps that accompany the text have been prepared solely for the convenience of readers; the designations and presentation of material in them do not imply the expression of any opinion whatsoever on the part of the World Bank, its affiliates, or its Board or member countries concerning the legal status of any country, territory, city, or area or of the authorities thereof or concerning the delimitation of its boundaries or its national affiliation.

The complete backlist of publications from the World Bank is shown in the annual *Index of Publications*, which contains an alphabetical title list (with full ordering information) and indexes of subjects, authors, and countries and regions. The latest edition is available free of charge from the Distribution Unit, Office of the Publisher, Department F, The World Bank, 1818 H Street, N.W., Washington, D.C. 20433, U.S.A., or from Publications, The World Bank, 66, avenue d'Iéna, 75116 Paris, France.

ISSN: 0253-7494

Mike Speirs is an agricultural development economist with Danagro. Ole Olsen is a senior agronomist with broad international experience and Danagro Adviser's chief agricultural consultant.

Library of Congress Cataloging-in-Publication Data

Speirs, Mike, 1956–
Indigenous integrated farming systems in the Sahel / Mike Speirs, Ole Olsen.
p. cm.—(World Bank technical paper, ISSN 0253-7494 ; 179)
(Africa Technical Department series)
Includes bibliographical references.
ISBN 0-8213-2180-3
1. Traditional farming—Sahel. 2. Agriculture—Economic aspects—Sahel. 3. Rural development—Sahel. 4. Sahel—Economic policy. I. Olsen, Ole, 1942– . II. Title. III. Series. IV. Series: World Bank technical paper. Africa Technical Department series.
GN645.S67 1992 92-20634
CIP

Foreword

This paper presents the results of a study examining the development of mixed farming systems in the Sahelian region of West Africa. The study was part of a program of research into the future directions of livestock production, agricultural development, and resource management in Sub-Saharan Africa, carried out by the Agriculture Division of the World Bank's Africa Technical Department. The Danish International Development Agency (DANIDA) provided funds for the study and contributed to the work of the consultants and researchers.

Although it is widely recognized that crop and livestock production in the Sahelian countries is in crisis, the full implications for human welfare, the sustainability of farming systems, and environmental degradation are inadequately appreciated. The population explosion in recent decades is at the root of the crisis, but it is exacerbated by low rainfall, droughts, and infertile fragile soils. The process is characterized by the breakdown of pastoral systems, settlement, and the rapid adoption of integrated crop/livestock systems by traditional crop farmers and settled pastoralists. It is influenced by many factors, the most important being a scarcity of land for crops and grazing. Other factors include the difficult economic environment, changing aspirations and behavior patterns, fragile ecological conditions, and political marginalization of the cultivators and pastoralists.

This study describes the evolution of integrated crop and livestock systems and the underlying causal factors. Particular attention is given to the allocation of resources, especially land and labor, among different crop and animal production activities. The factors that determine the adoption of animal traction, the use of manure and crop residues in farming systems, and the pattern of income generation in households are analyzed and discussed. The study concludes that present farming systems are unsustainable in the long term. Appropriate strategies are recommended to reduce the identified constraints.

The challenge now is to implement these strategies to reduce environmental degradation and improve the welfare of farmers and pastoralists to the greatest possible extent.

Ismail Serageldin
Director
Technical Department
Africa Region
World Bank
May 1992

Acknowledgments

This study was undertaken under the auspices of the World Bank. It was initiated and managed by Poul Sihm, Senior Livestock Specialist in the Bank's Africa Technical Department. Funding for the study was contributed by the Danish International Development Agency (DANIDA) and it was conducted by a consulting firm, Carl Bro International. Valuable support and assistance was provided by the Bank's Environmental Department.

A number of descriptive and analytic reports were written by a team of consultants working with Carl Bro International: Charles Gooch, Preben Haugaard, Robert Lallemand, and Henrik Secher Marcussen. Their work was based on case studies undertaken by a team of students from Roskilde University Centre in Denmark. These students, Tine Bensaoula, Tove Degnbol, Dorrit Jensen, Christian Lund, Henrik Nielsen, and Klaus Sall, were assisted by local personnel including Khady Dial, Boubacar Fall, Tapsir Ndao, and Abdoulaye Sy (Senegal); Youssouf Diabaté (Mali); Philippe Bamago, Zakaria Gnégné, and Bégué Sessouma (Burkina Faso) and Moussa Assane, Soumana Assane, and Aboubacar Hamidon (Niger).

This final report is based on the original study reports and other documents, taking into account comments and editorial advice given by team members, by John Ashley, by staff in the Agricultural and Environmental Divisions of the World Bank's Africa Technical Department, by John English, Environmental Department, and World Bank staff in the Africa Region. Many useful comments on an earlier draft were made by Roy Behnke (Overseas Development Institute, London), Anders Hjort af Ornas (Scandinavian Institute of African Studies, Uppsala), Ralph von Kaufmann (International Livestock Center for Africa, Addis Ababa), and F. Riveros (FAO, Rome). The photographs were taken by Tove Degnbol.

The authors are indebted to all those mentioned for their contributions to this publication. We also wish to thank Michael Walshe, Paula Strawhecker, Alicia Hetzner, Muriel Prah and Christina Dhanaraj for their input into the final stages of the study.

Contents

Abbreviations and Acronyms

CFA	Franc de la Communauté Financière Africaine
CILSS	Comité Inter-Etats de Lutte Contre la Sécheresse au Sahel
CMDT	Compagnie Malienne du Développment de Textiles
CRPA	Centre Régional de Production Agro-Pastorale (Burkina Faso)
EC	European Community
FAO	Food and Agriculture Organization of the United Nations
ICRISAT	International Crop Research Institute for the Semi-Arid Tropics
IFAD	International Fund for Agricultural Development
ILCA	International Livestock Centre for Africa
IMF	International Monetary Fund
ISRA	Institut Sénégalais de la Recherche Agricole
NGO	Non-governmental organization
OACV	Opération Arachière et Culture Vivrière (Senegal)
OECD	Organization for Economic Cooperation and Development
ONCAD	Office Nationale de Coopération et d'Assistance au Développement (Senegal)
SODEVA	Société de Développement et de Vulgarization Agricole (Senegal)
SOFITEX	Société des Fibres Textiles (Burkina Faso)
TLU	Tropical Livestock Unit
USAID	United States Agency for International Development

Exchange Rates

The CFA franc is convertible at a fixed rate of 50 CFAF to 1 FF. The average exchange rates of the CFA franc to the US dollar during the study period were:

1987: 301 CFA = US$1
1988: 298 CFA = US$1
1989: 330 CFA = US$1

Summary

Aims

The principal objective of this study was to examine alternative ways through which the integration of animal production with crop production could contribute to an intensification of both food and cash crop production and encourage the maintenance of soil fertility in the Sahelian region of West Africa. The study was therefore designed to assess the potential role of livestock in integrated farming systems (mixed farming), focusing on the technical constraints as well as social factors and the economic incentives for livestock production and animal products.

Methodology - Country Studies

The study was carried out in several phases which included the collection and analysis of data and information from selected households and villages in Burkina Faso, Mali, Niger, and Senegal. The areas studied are located in the Sahelo-Sudanian and Sudanian agro-climatic zones of West Africa where average annual rainfall is between 400mm and 900mm. Agricultural production in these areas is characterized by modest and highly variable crop yields, where fluctuations in precipitation, recurrent droughts and increasing environmental degradation are significant limiting factors. Declining soil fertility in areas where fallow periods have become shorter (or have disappeared altogether), linked to an expansion of the area under cultivation, pose major problems for the sustainability of farming systems in the Sahel.

Case studies in selected villages revealed the complex dynamics of these processes, and illustrated some of the strategies which have been adopted by different groups of crop cultivators and pastoralists to maintain production and income. The allocation of resources, particularly land, between different crop and livestock production activities, the adoption of techniques such as animal traction, the use of manure and crop residues, and the patterns of income generation and distribution in the households and rural communities, formed the focal points of these studies. **Annex 1** outlines some of the methodological difficulties encountered during the various phases.

Economic and Socio-Cultural Factors

The economic policies pursued by the governments of the region during the 1980s, based on the notion of structural adjustment designed to reduce budgetary and balance of payments deficits and to change the structure of production in order to produce tradeable goods in greater quantities, have had various effects on the farming systems in the areas studied. Public expenditure cuts and the withdrawal of parastatal agencies from the agricultural sector have resulted in increased input costs and reduced extension services and credit facilities, which have not been compensated by increases in the prices of crops and livestock. The deterioration in the terms of trade of agricultural products from the Sahel, notably groundnuts and cotton which are important sources of export earnings in Senegal and Burkina Faso, has been compounded by increased competition in West African livestock markets.

Infrastructure and agricultural marketing systems are poor, and liberalization through structural adjustment does not appear to have resulted in any significant increases in output. The good harvests in the second half of the 1980s were reflected in a rapid decline in cereals prices, which acted as a further disincentive to on-farm investment. With the exception of the cotton farmers in Burkina Faso, returns to land and labor for the main crops grown in the villages studied were very low. Nevertheless, wide variations in levels of income, wealth and household size were found in all villages.

Cash incomes from crops were largely limited to the groundnut and cotton producing households. Many farmers did not produce enough cereals to meet their domestic requirements. More and more emphasis is given to income diversification and all farmers in the villages studied in Mali, Niger and Senegal had some off-farm income sources, mostly remittances from migrant workers. Only cotton farmers in Burkina Faso were mainly dependent on crop revenues. However a process of income polarization was observed, with richer farmers increasing their assets while poorer farmers were often obliged to sell off their assets during drought periods. Some of these poorer farmers have given up trying to make a living from agriculture, and have joined the rural exodus. The introduction of draft animals appears to have contributed to this polarization of incomes since they have permitted some farmers to make a substantial increase in cultivated areas, notably in the cash crop zones.

Some of the villages retained a high degree of social cohesion and homogeneity. Others, notably those where large numbers of immigrants have settled in recent years leading to considerable social and ethnic heterogeneity, were characterized by conflicts particularly in relation to the most valuable asset, namely land. The dynamics of social cohesion and differentiation in the villages entail the maintenance and the breakdown of exchange systems in different contexts which affect access, not only to land, but also to other resources including labor, equipment, and draft animals. Social relations in terms of time spent working for other farmers and the borrowing of equipment are also important factors in the process of socio-economic differentiation.

Integration - Trends and Issues

The shortage of land has become the major production constraint in all the villages which were surveyed. Competition for land takes three forms: between crop use and pasture use, between crop land for residents and crop land for immigrants, and between pasture for village livestock and pasture for transhumant livestock. Under prevailing land tenure conditions in the Sahel, usufruct rights to land are allocated to cultivators, and thus crop land takes priority over pasture, and the best pasture lands are progressively lost to cultivation. Immigrants can only obtain usufruct rights to land where there is sufficient for both residents and immigrants. Borrowing land is frequent but often leads to conflict when the owner wishes to reclaim it. Residual uncultivated land is available for communal grazing, but by common law of precedent, village livestock has priority access to it over transhumant livestock because it is still village land. Village boundaries in the areas studied are contiguous and there is no unclaimed land between villages.

The process of integrating livestock into crop production systems is initiated when cultivable land becomes scarce in relation to population. Instead of two complementary production systems interacting through the exchange of by-products (manure and crop residues) and factors of production (labor), integration takes place as competition for the main production factor, land, becomes increasingly significant. Crop farmers require increasing quantities of manure to fertilize the soil of "old" arable land which has been steadily depleted of nutrients and organic matter as fallow periods have declined and cropping intensity has increased. Pastoralists are faced with reduced pastures as the best areas are brought under cultivation, and they then become progressively more dependent on crop residues for feed. Intensification of livestock production also occurs as more animals (both large and small ruminants) are maintained at or near households where they are fed on crop residues and straw collected from the fields. Manure from these animals is increasingly used on the fields. The introduction of draft animals has further accelerated the process of integration by contributing to an expansion of cropping through a major increase in cultivated areas.

The use of manure in the villages studied was strongly contingent on the reduction of fallow periods, as few farmers were able to keep land under fallow for more than five years in comparison with the twenty year fallow periods which were common in the past. Similarly, the use of crop residues is assuming greater importance as production from natural pastures declines. Practices such as the collection, transport and storage of crop residues are increasing, and fodder markets are now widespread in the areas studied.

The use of draft animals for cultivation has been negatively affected by the low level of farmgate crop prices as well as by higher equipment and feed costs. In the areas studied in Senegal and Mali, the use of draft animals for cultivation was declining and donkeys were replacing oxen for traction purposes. But oxen were extensively used on the more profitable cotton farms in Burkina Faso. Given the arid conditions and low levels of production in the villages studied in Niger, cultivation with draft animals is rare. However, the use of the same animals both for traction and transportation (notably donkeys) is on the increase in the areas studied. Decreasing benefits from their use in cultivation can be offset by gains from their use in the transport of inputs, crop residues, manure and products to markets.

Development Scenarios and Recommendations

The issues of access to land, usufruct rights and security of tenure are of fundamental importance in efforts to develop integrated farming systems, and to maintain pastoral zones in the Sahel in the context of high population growth rates. Sustainable production of food and cash crops as well as livestock and animal products are threatened by over exploitation of land and by the degradation of soils and pastures. The introduction of land use management schemes to ensure rational use of resources is essential, as part of a process by which farmers and pastoralists are able to increase their incomes through the integration and intensification of production. Nevertheless, there is severe pressure on available natural resources, and it is not easy to improve land use management practices in the face of high population growth rates, although various pilot schemes have been carried out with some success in some areas. Reform of land tenure legislation is an important step in this process. The fertility of soils in the Sahel is continually declining as a result of the reduced, and in some areas total, abandonment of fallow periods. Neither minerals nor organic matter are replaced in the soil and the quantities of manure at present being applied are totally inadequate to sustain recurrent crop yields let alone improve them. It is not theoretically possible to maintain nutrient or organic matter levels unless there are substantial pasture or forest areas from which organic matter can be transferred either directly to the fields as compost, or processed through livestock to generate more manure.

In the course of this study it was estimated that with present production systems about twenty-three hectares of natural pasture would be required to produce sufficient manure to maintain constant organic matter levels in the soil on one hectare for continuous cropping. Such expansive pasture areas are not available in the cropping zone of the Sahel, and even if they were, the practice would be unworkable and unsustainable. The introduction of legume fallows, although potentially providing a technical solution to this problem, would deprive many farmers of land for immediate food crop production, and would thus have serious social consequences. Selective use of fertilizers, coupled with enhanced soil and water conservation schemes, may be important options in this respect. But the inescapable conclusion is that under the prevailing land use conditions the land and soil resources in the areas studied cannot support the present human and animal populations.

There have also been major changes in the pattern of livestock ownership. It appears that an increasing proportion of stock in the Sahel is now owned by crop farmers, who invested their surplus revenue from crop sales in animal production when crop prices were higher. They have also profited from low livestock prices during droughts to acquire more animals from poorer farmers or pastoralists. Although providing manure and draft for their fields, the livestock are principally maintained as a capital reserve which can be called on in an emergency. Although the maintenance of such livestock contributes to the overstocking of pastures and to land degradation, there is also a trend towards production intensification by keeping more animals near households.

Pastures in the crop zone are increasingly utilized by village-based livestock to the detriment of the transhumant herds. This factor plus the declining area and productivity of pastures as the best land is brought under cultivation, has led to increases in the demand for crop residues for feed, which were previously available for transhumant herds but are now largely consumed by village-based stock. Many transhumant herds are moving south where crop residue output and pasture production are higher but where the risk of contracting diseases such as trypanosomiasis is greater. But even here the scope for obtaining dry season feed is declining. Thus there appear to be two longer term trends. On the one hand, despite the difficulties, mixed farming systems are developing in the southern (Sudano-Guinean) zones. North of the cultivation limit (350 mm annual rainfall isohyet) where intensive arable farming is scarcely feasible, predominantly pastoral production systems prevail. Traditional transhumant herding between these zones is becoming increasingly difficult.

The process of social stratification has been accentuated by changes in the farming systems of the Sahel. The study revealed that there is considerable diversity both between households in each village and between villages. Many of the poorer villagers have been gradually forced to abandon farming and to seek a livelihood as migrant laborers in the towns and in the coastal cities of West Africa. Major variations in economic conditions within and between villages, which result from resource, infrastructural, social and political differences, imply a need for more location-specific development planning, backed up by the introduction of cost effective on-farm techniques to maximize the potential benefits from integration of crop and livestock production efforts.

The scope and limits of different techniques to improve soil fertility and increase the production of animal fodder were explored in the study, and it was emphasized that the economic viability of intensive mixed farming systems in the Sahel depends on the implementation of appropriate national and regional policies to support the development of the agricultural sector. Some specific proposals include:

a. As a first step, every emphasis should be given to programs designed to allocate land rights to farmers and pastoralists who could then be assisted in the planning and implementing of rational land use schemes, including ensuring access to grazing land and water supplies.

b. To tackle the problem of soil fertility, the vigorous promotion of more efficient manure use and composing techniques, together with the application of inorganic fertilizer, is essential, although this will only be viable in an improved economic environment.

c. Increasing farmers' incomes through the promotion of integration necessitates measures to encourage the production of fodder, and schemes to enhance the intensive fattening of stock wherever possible given the economic constraints.

d. Further provision of draft animals and carts should only be undertaken after careful assessment of the overall demand for transport in relation to the existing supply of draft animals and carts, since it would be easy to saturate the market.

e. Further investment in teaching animal husbandry techniques to farmers and pastoralists in the region may be important.

f. Finally, a number of supplementary measures, directed at improving the organization and methods by which savings and credit, extension services, crop marketing, and inputs are supplied, could be highly beneficial. Efforts should be undertaken to promote improved processing and distribution of animal products in West Africa.

1. *Background of the Study*

The development and sustainability of agriculture in the Sahel is thought to depend, to a great extent, on the integration of livestock in crop production systems.[1] The principal objective of this study was to examine alternative ways through which the integration of animal production with crop production systems could encourage intensification of food and cash crop production and the associated maintenance of soil fertility. Both livestock development and intensified crop production are of great importance to the economies of the countries in this region of Africa. But numerous problems must be confronted to develop sustainable farming systems, some of which have been analyzed in the course of this study.

Traditional farming systems in the Sahel have been based on an adaptation to low and variable rainfall, poor and fragile soils and widely available land. These extensive land-use systems were characterized by low productivity per hectare and high levels of crop yield variability. But, to quote Matlon (1987), in recent years:

> growing populations are upsetting this ecological balance by cultivating more marginal soils and by continuous cultivation. Increased cash needs are also inducing farmers in some areas to put greater resources into cash crop production, often employing technologies that accelerate a decline in soil quality. The immediate result is nearly stagnant growth in yields of food crops and a general fall in aggregate farm output per rural inhabitant. A more pervasive long-term effect in areas of greatest population density is the steady decline of the natural resource base (p.75).

In the livestock sector, the severe droughts of the 1970s and early 1980s accentuated the difficulties faced by pastoral animal production systems in the Sahel. High levels of animal mortality, distress sales at low prices, migration southwards and reductions in the weight of the animals and in herders' incomes, as well as falling export earnings characterized the progressive breakdown of a sector where livestock activities have steadily exceeded the optimum limits set by the natural resources. The over exploitation of grazing land and resulting environmental degradation, coupled with the tendency to leave less land fallow and the rapid expansion of areas under crop cultivation, has threatened the viability of pastoral production systems (Club du Sahel/CILSS, 1988, pp. 2-4).

The greater integration of cultivation and livestock production systems is increasingly seen as a means of conserving a minimum of dry season grazing land, restoring rangelands in the pastoral areas of the Sahel, improving the production of animal feed, and maintaining the productivity of food and cash crop production systems through improvements in soil fertility. An understanding of these processes necessitates analyses of various ecological, economic, and socio-cultural factors. This study was therefore designed to assess the potential role of livestock in integrated farming systems (mixed farming), through an examination of the technical applicability of integrating livestock in farming systems, as well as of the system of economic incentives for livestock production and animal products.

It was anticipated that the study would throw some light on a wide range of related issues. These included (a) the comparative advantage of livestock in the economy, (b) the economic environment for livestock production nationally and regionally, (c) whether 'integration' (the transformation of the traditional agricultural production system into a mixed farming system) or 'interaction' (finding ways of reviving the classical manure contracting system) should be promoted, (d) the problem of year-round keeping of livestock in villages (the management of herds, protection of crops, stock water supplies and manpower), (e) the difficulty of transforming traditional modes of production, (f) institutional reorganization required to provide maximum support for the system, (g) the legislation required, (h) education and training, (i) agricultural credit, (j) the distortions and inefficiencies in the marketing system, (k) pricing policies, (l) the role of the private sector, and (m) the input supply system. All of these subjects are considered, but the focus is on the main results of the study, emphasizing the contradictions which are encountered in the development of integrated farming systems in the Sahel.

Approach and Methodology

The study was undertaken in several phases between 1986 and 1989. A literature search was carried out at relevant institutions, and discussions were held with professional staff at research institutions working in livestock and crop production in the Sahel. Among the issues identified at this stage, it emerged that there are several different interpretations of the rationale for the adoption of mixed farming.[2] Although there are considerable benefits to be gained from integrating crop cultivation and livestock raising, there are also many constraints which have limited the impact of efforts to develop mixed farming systems in this region of Africa. Thus, while there are various ways in which crop cultivation and livestock production are complementary (crop residues can be used as animal feed, the animals can provide manure and be used for traction purposes), the two systems also compete with each other (notably for land use and labor inputs).

It is important to note that the two key terms used in this study, interaction and integration can be defined as follows. Separate crop and livestock production systems **interact** through an inter-group exchange of by-products or production factors, where, for example, crop residues and manure are exchanged and used by different groups of herders and crop cultivators. **Integration** occurs through complementary production activities on an individual farm or group of farms, where, for example, farming in a "mixed" way uses crop residues to feed the livestock and their manure to fertilize the fields.

First phase

Following this survey of previous investigations of crop and livestock production integration, suitable areas for case studies in four selected West African countries, Burkina Faso, Mali, Niger and Senegal, were identified.[3] A general picture of the production systems and socio-economic characteristics of the areas was then obtained during the first phase field studies, which also focused on the identification of production constraints and possible indigenous solutions. After a number of villages were selected for detailed study, a questionnaire was prepared for household interviews to determine the main crop and livestock production activities of each household, the extent of both integration and interaction and the ownership and management of livestock, as well as the social structure and economic basis of the household. Certain key issues were emphasized in this initial survey, such as the use of manure and crop residues. The questionnaire was adapted to fit the conditions in each area, and interviews were carried out with between fifteen and thirty households in each of the selected villages.

Samples of the livestock herds were also monitored to assess the herd composition and the production strategies used by the owners. An impression of the livestock movements in the study areas was also gained. The collection of data on the herds continued throughout the first year of the study. Furthermore, the prices of crops and livestock products as well as production inputs and basic food items were collected at village markets. Finally, interviews with a number of influential people such as civil servants and village leaders were carried out in order to substantiate the information gathered in the villages and to offer a wider perspective on the development issues in the areas.

An examination of the results of these surveys led to the identification of several significant issues (a) the effects of interaction and integration on the process of extension of the cultivated area as opposed to intensification of production, and (b) the scope and limits for households in different socio-economic categories in terms of their participation in, and adoption of, integration activities.

Second phase

These issues were further analyzed in the subsequent second phase field studies, which concentrated on assessing the contribution of animal traction to expansion, the impact of this process on soil fertility, and the extent to which the use of animal manure counteracts losses in soil fertility. Does the process of integration between crop and livestock production promote or hinder the expansion of land use?

The correlation between socio-economic groups and integration activities was assessed, as well as the extent to which the adoption of integration practices could improve the incomes of the poorer households. Is there a direct correlation between the socio-economic situation of a household and the degree to which it practices crop and livestock integration? Is integration a realistic and effective means of improving the income levels of the poor households?

The scope of the study was also broadened by including more villages within the same study region in each country. Possible forms of intervention which could contribute to overcoming the constraints which restrict the adoption of mixed farming in the Sahel were also identified.

Overall development trends were linked to household investment strategies and compared with the relative success of different households. A more detailed understanding of the factors which affect household investment patterns was obtained, through which the consequences of different investment strategies in terms of household income could be assessed.

Greater emphasis was placed on examining the range of socio-economic stratification amongst the households and the reasons for the variation observed, rather than focusing on an average household. A more detailed understanding of integration practices was obtained by specific on-farm monitoring of a few selected crops. Finally, given the difficulties encountered in collecting reliable quantitative input and output data during the first phase field studies, greater emphasis was placed on gathering qualitative information.

Four to six villages at different stages of development and displaying different degrees of crop and livestock production integration were selected in order to examine six key subject areas: (a) social and economic characteristics as well as credit systems, (b) farming and integration practices, (c) livestock management systems, (d) interactions, (e) land tenure systems, and (f) local organization and development schemes. Information was gathered through interviews with civil servants, local leaders, research personnel and extension service officers, through group meetings at village level, through guided interviews with ten to fifteen selected households in each village, and through in-depth interviews with members of a few selected households. Given the difficulties of collecting accurate figures on yields, manure inputs, and other production factors, contacts with other professional personnel in the four countries were broadened so that information from other sources could be used to supplement the findings of the study.

The complexity of the ecological and social processes which influence change in the farming systems of the region, and the problems of data collection and analysis, mean that the quality of the information on which the conclusions and recommendations are based varies a good deal.[4]

2. *Description of the Areas Studied*

Location and General Characteristics

The areas studied in Senegal, Mali, Burkina Faso and Niger are shown on the **Map** and their location described in detail in **Annex 2**. The map also indicates the overall agro-ecological zonal classification of this region of West Africa.

Climate

The amount and distribution of precipitation is of fundamental importance to the development of agriculture in the Sahel. The areas studied are located in different zones according to the standard fao agro-climatic zonal classification (as shown in the map and in **Table 1**).

This agro-climatic zonation is based on isohyets derived from rainfall data for the period from 1931 to 1960 when relatively abundant precipitation levels were recorded. Using rainfall data for the period from 1961 to the mid-1980s the isohyets would be further south. Since the mid-1960s there has been a marked decrease in average annual rainfall of between 100 mm and 200 mm throughout the semi-arid region of West Africa with the greatest decline occurring in the wetter zones. The general trend towards increasing aridity in the region gives rise to considerable concern. There are various explanations of the causes of this process, while recurrent droughts have accentuated the pressure exerted by human activities on the fragile environment.[5]

The rainfall in the areas studied is unimodal with one long dry season of eight to nine months. Temperatures are high, with mean monthly maximum temperatures between 34° and $45^{o}C$ and minimum temperatures between 11° and $24^{o}C$. The variations in rainfall contribute to major differences in agricultural production in terms of the choice of crops, input levels and average yields (Table 1).

Soils, Vegetation, and Agriculture

The soils in all the areas studied are very sandy (80 percent or more) with an extremely low organic matter content (less than 1 percent). The soils are acid (below pH 6) with rapid mineralization of organic

Table 1. Rainfall and Climatic Zones

Country	*Average annual rainfall in area of study (mm)*	*Climatic zone*
Senegal	500-700	Sahelo-Sudanian /Sudanian
Mali	550-650	Sahelo-Sudanian /Sudanian
Burkina Faso	850-950	Sudano-Guinean
Niger	400-500	Sahelo-Sudanian

Source: Country studies, Gorse and Steeds (1987)

matter, light in structure and weak in water retention capacity. From a chemical point of view the soils have a low buffer capacity and are deficient in phosphorus and nitrogen. In most places a hard pan of laterite, often not far below the soil surface, makes the layer of cultivable soil very thin, which is another reason for the very low water retention capacity. As a consequence the vegetation is poor, with few varieties of *Gramineae* in particular.

Crop production is characterized by normally modest and highly variable yields. In the villages studied in Senegal and Burkina Faso, farmers grow cash crops, groundnuts in Senegal and cotton in Burkina Faso, for which there are assured markets with fixed prices. No cash crops are grown by farmers in the villages studied in Mali and Niger. All farmers in all the villages grow cereal crops for domestic consumption. Millet, and to a much lesser extent, sorghum, is grown in Senegal. In Mali, millet is also the predominant staple foodgrain usually intercropped with cowpeas. In Burkina Faso, where the villages have a wetter climate, sorghum is the principal cereal, while in Niger millet usually intercropped with cowpeas is grown.

Figure 1 presents some aggregate production, cultivation area, and average yield data for cereals output in the four countries during the 1980s. Following poor or mediocre harvests of the early 1980s, total output increased significantly in most countries after 1985. Nevertheless, much of this increase has been attributed to an extension of the cultivated area, and average yields per hectare have remained low in the Sahelian zone (particularly in Niger), while they appear to be on the increase, given adequate precipitation, in the Sudanian zones (notably in southern Mali).

Population

The estimated total population of the villages in the areas studied in the four countries is shown in **Table 2**. In **Senegal**, the predominant ethnic group is the Wolof, but there are a number of other ethnic groups; the area has been subject to considerable immigration over the past sixty years. Immigrants continue to settle in the northern villages. The villages which were studied in **Mali** are dominated by the Bambara and there are only a few people of other ethnic groups such as the Fulani and the Marka; there has been no immigration into these villages within the past twenty years.

In **Burkina Faso**, four out of the five villages studied have been subject to massive immigration by the Mossi from the central plateau; the Bobo are indigenous to the area but they only predominate in Selenkoro. In the villages of Bankouma, Kouroumani and, Kouka the Mossi are the largest ethnic group. Other ethnic groups include the Fulani, the Dafing, the Samogo, and the Bambara.

In **Niger**, the villages have all been subject to varying degrees of immigration due to the drought, which has forced people to leave more marginal areas in the north. Karakara and Zabori are almost entirely inhabited by the Haussa, but Tesa is entirely Djerma; the village of Birniel Alfari is a settlement of Fulani; the two villages studied in the first phase, Dokimana and Teroudje, are inhabited by Djerma and Fulani respectively.

With the exception of the Fulani who were to be found in all areas studied, and a few Maure in Senegal, all other ethnic groups are primarily arable farmers, though with varying degrees of livestock ownership. The Fulani traditionally practice transhumant livestock systems, and the Maure nomadic livestock systems, although in many of the study villages they are settled and practice arable farming.

Characteristics of the Areas Studied

Senegal

The district of Koungheul where the villages studied are located, forms part of the groundnut basin which stretches from

Figure 1. Cereals Production Area, Output and Yield per Hectare

Senegal:

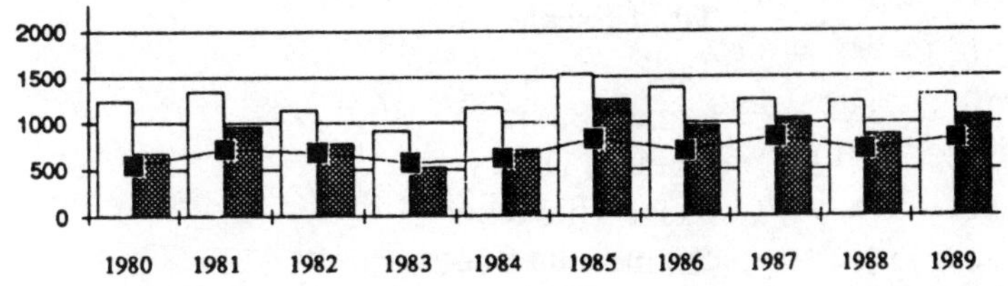

Mali:

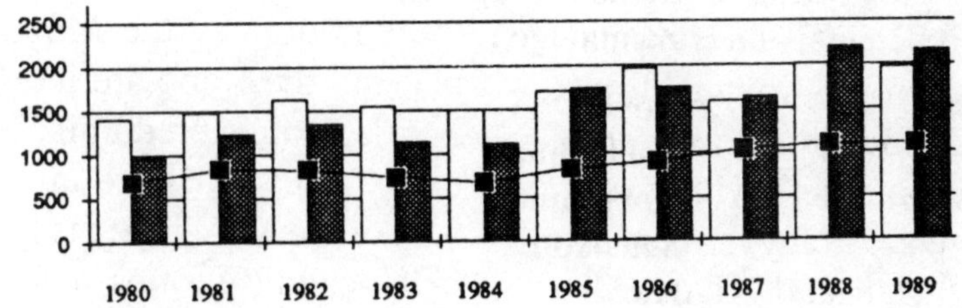

Burkina Faso:

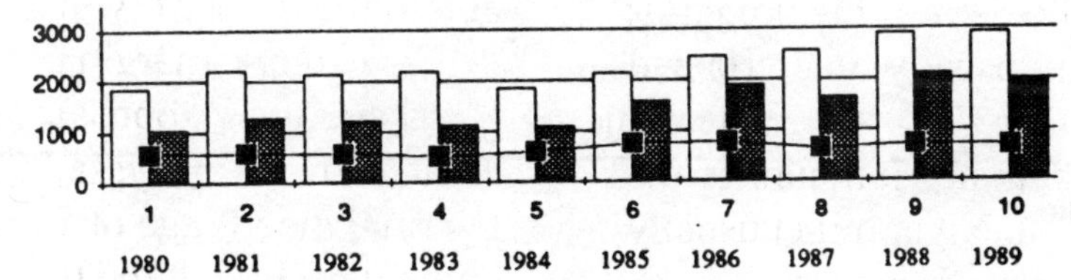

Niger:

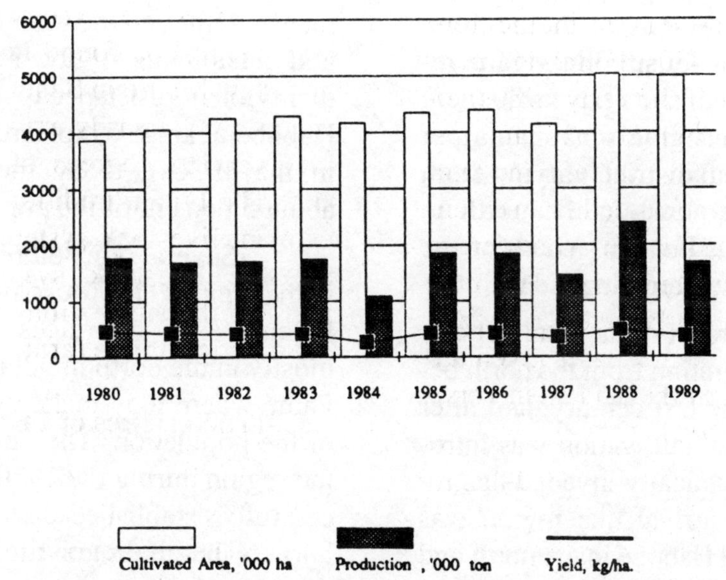

Source: FAO Production Yearbooks and Club du Sahel/CILSS data

Table 2. Population in the Villages Studied

Country	*Village*	*Population*
Senegal	Tibot Escale	900
	Taïf	700
	Gainth Pathé	1000
	Ngouye Dierry	1500
	Fasse Thiékène	700
	Koumbidia Socé	500
Mali	Boussin	2200
	Sakoiba	700
	Toko	500
	Somonodougouni	1000
	Zambougou	500
Burkina Faso	Kouka	8600
	Bankouma	1900
	Kouroumani	900
	Selenkoro	500
	Kié	approx. 1200
Niger	Tesa	1800
	Birniel Alfari	approx. 500
	Karakara	1700
	Zabori	not known
	Dokimani	700
	Teroudje	400

Source: Country studies

the densely populated Sine, Baol, Diourbel and Thies regions in the west to the Saloum region and to part of Sénégal Oriental in the central and eastern regions of the country. While the population density in the Sine region is over 100 inhabitants per km}, there are only about twenty-five inhabitants per km} in the Koungheul district, varying from eight inhabitants per km} in the north to thirty-five inhabitants per km} south of the road from Kaolack to Tambacounda.

About 90 percent of the total population are Wolof. Emigration from the north began at the turn of the last century, and after 1930 when groundnut cultivation was introduced, the Wolof practically invaded this region. Prior to their arrival, the region was inhabited by the Peul Habobé in the north and by the Mandingue in the south.[6] Since the drought years of the 1970s, an increasing number of Fulani have settled in their former dry season camps, either in Wolof dominated villages or by establishing their own settlements. Although the Mandingue are the original inhabitants of the region, and despite their violent resistance together with the Peul Habobé against Wolof immigration (notably in the 1930s), today they constitute only about 5 percent of the population.

Several other ethnic groups are found in the region. The Toucouleurs are offspring of Fulani-Wolof marriages who have settled mostly in the north in villages such as Gainth Pathé where they make up about 20 percent of the population. The Peul Fouta arrived in the region during the 1960s and have so successfully established themselves as charcoal burners that their activities represent a major threat to the forestry resources. The Maure are mostly transhumant pastoralists like the

Peul Habobé. A limited number of Bambara from Mali have made the transition from seasonal laborers to settled farmers in the region. Finally some Seerer have moved into the area in recent years, under the pressure of extreme land scarcity in the Sine region, and have rented land in the northern zones.

Thus, acting as a buffer zone between the densely populated areas to the north, south, east, and west, the continued inflow of migrants has resulted in increasing problems of land scarcity. The relatively harmonious relations between the different ethnic groups in the past are gradually giving way to conflicts, particularly as disputes over land rights become more frequent. New arrivals have great difficulties in obtaining land.

An estimated 60 percent of the total land area is cultivated. The non-cultivable land, where lateritic soils are found, is used as pasture for the cattle and small ruminants during the rainy season and at the beginning of the dry season. South of the main road however, the vegetation on these soils provides such poor fodder that only the protected forests *(forêts classés)* and hollows can be grazed. Apart from the lateritic soils, *sol doir*, *sol deck* and *sol deck-doir* predominate. The *sol doir* are sandy soils found in the north, while *sol deck* are soils with a higher clay content which account for 50 percent of the soils in the south.

According to official statistics, groundnuts are grown on about 50 percent of the cultivated land in the region. Millet accounts for a further 45 percent of the cultivated land, and the remaining 5 percent is used for the cultivation of sorghum, maize, cassava, and cowpeas. Cotton was also grown until the mid-1970s, but marketing difficulties brought an end to production.

The typical crop pattern is based on a zonal division around each village comprising the inner fields *(champs de case)* and bush fields *(champs de brousse)*. Millet is intensively grown on the fields close to the village using manure as fertilizer, but without crop rotation or fallow periods. Groundnuts alternate with millet or sorghum on the fields in the bush, where, if possible, the land is left fallow in a three year cycle. Fallow periods have almost completely disappeared in the south since the end of the 1970s, and the crop rotation now is groundnuts followed by millet/sorghum. Maize is cultivated in hollows or sometimes on part of an inner field, and cassava is usually cultivated in the household yards.

In addition to crop cultivation, farmers practice animal husbandry in varying degrees. A wealthy minority own cattle herds, and most farmers have small ruminants and one or more draft animals. Curiously, poultry raising is almost non-existent. All the animals are kept on the farm throughout the year. There was a tradition of outherding in the past, but this appears to have ceased due to the risk of theft. The cattle are herded by the Fulani during the rainy season, who take the animals up to ten kilometers from the village returning with them every night for "parking" either on the fallow land if such is available or as close as possible to the fields in the bush. During the dry season (from mid-January to mid-June) the cattle are put out to graze on the stubble.

Similarly the small ruminants are kept in herds near the settlements during the rainy season and released to graze during the dry season. In general the *chef du village* organizes all the small ruminants of each village in one single herd (sometimes two if they are numerous) and everybody pays the herders according to the number of animals he possesses. Furthermore, the small ruminants are kept in enclosures in the yards around the family houses at night throughout the year. Most farmers transport the manure from these enclosures to the nearest arable fields during May, prior to sowing.

The most common draft animal is the horse which has been used since the mid-1960s when sowing and hoeing machines were introduced. South of the road, is relatively widespread, while in most northern villages this practice is employed by only six to eight households per village. Donkeys, generally regarded locally as despicable animals, are used for transport and for cultivation work by those farmers who cannot afford to buy a pair of oxen or a horse.

The oxen and horses are kept in enclosures during the rainy season when they are working, and, as noted above, most farmers transport the manure to the millet fields in May. Groundnut haulms are the main fodder resource. These are stacked and stored after the harvest and given as daily rations to the animals in the enclosures during the rainy season. Farmers who have sufficient fodder also keep their horses and oxen in the enclosures during the dry season. No crops are cultivated specifically as fodder in this region.

According to official statistics, it is estimated that about 90 percent of the people in the region are farmers whose livelihood is based on variations of the above farming system. The majority of the remaining 10 percent are pastoralists (mostly Fulani) who regard themselves as livestock herders rather than crop cultivators. Nevertheless, although their earnings from livestock sales are often much greater than from the sale of crops, most of them cultivate a few hectares of millet and groundnuts.

Finally there is a rapidly disappearing group of transhumant pastoralists. In the past, milk and manure were often exchanged for crop residues and millet throughout the region, but now the pastoralists are found only in villages with abundant water resources in the dry season (notably those with wells). Exceptionally however, during the drought years at the beginning of the 1980s even those villages with insufficient water resources were visited by pastoralists from the Ferlo, Louga and Djolof regions (in the north and east).

Only the poorest and the wealthiest households depend more on non-agricultural incomes than on their income from the sale of groundnuts. Commerce and transport are the most common sources of additional income for "average" households, while the poorer farmers earn money through the sale of commodities from the bush such as firewood, charcoal and hay. But the relative prosperity of this groundnut based region has been affected by many changes during the 1980s.

The agricultural policy introduced in 1980 made groundnut production increasingly difficult. In short, subsidized credit for the purchase of seed, fertilizer, equipment and draft animals was withdrawn, while trade was liberalized. While the general level of mechanization during the 1970s was quite high and farmers rarely sowed, weeded, or harvested by hand, a process of demechanization is now underway in which farmers either share fewer tools or do the work by hand. The number of draft animals is also declining and the use of chemical fertilizer has become almost non-existent.[7]

The agricultural extension services have also undergone changes. Down to 1982, SODEVA employed one consultant for every ten to fifteen villages in the district, advising the farmers on systems, composting techniques, the upkeep and repair of equipment and so on. The efficiency of the extension services built up during the 1970s contributed to the farmers' extensive knowledge of ways and means to intensify agricultural production. The present extension service is divided into crop and livestock sections which do not attempt to introduce integration techniques. The number of staff has also been reduced, with only two people dealing with crop extension and five working on livestock production in the 321 villages of the district.

There are no externally financed projects in the region apart from a reforestation scheme with small plantations in selected villages. However a very dynamic local initiative known as the "Projet de Bamba" operates in forty-seven villages on the basis of a decentralized structure through which each sub-section at village level is independent and responsible for its own funds raised through member's savings. It was only after 1982-83 when the national extension service was reduced that this organization expanded, although it has existed since 1978. Market gardening schemes, small ruminant stock raising, reforestation and the organization of seed and equipment purchases are amongst the many activities of this movement, which has plans to expand and diversify in the future.

Finally, as far as infrastructure is concerned, the most serious problem is the lack of water in many villages. Geological conditions prevent the digging of wells by handtools, since these wells must be between sixty and ninety meters deep. On the other hand, the railway from Dakar to Bamako which reached Koungheul in 1912, has had a major effect on the development of the region, notably through the arrival of seasonal laborers from Mali. However, most local transport is provided by trucks and pick-up vans, although owners often charge high fees even for short distances. In the rainy season, most of the villages in the north are inaccessible by vehicle. Weekly markets are held in the larger villages, but in the others it is often difficult to obtain commodities such as vegetables, bread and meat. It is also sometimes difficult to find outlets for these goods and even the market in Koungheul is sometimes saturated. The only commodity that can always be sold is groundnuts, with the purchase organized through cooperatives using local storage in the major villages.

Mali

Ségou and the villages selected for this study are located in the fourth region of Mali, which, because of the good conditions for the production of millet, sorghum, and groundnuts, is known as the granary of the country. Nevertheless, the output of both cereals and groundnuts in this region has declined dramatically over the past ten years. Although rainfall usually averages nearly 700 mm per year, over the past fifteen years an annual average of less than 600 mm has frequently been recorded. The soils in the area investigated vary according to the topography, but all types, including sandy, sandy-loam, and loam soils are cultivated. Clay soils are found along the Niger river and in some shallow depressions in different areas.

The population density in this region is about twenty inhabitants per km}, and the annual average rate of population increase is approximately 2.5 percent. In terms of the ethnic composition, the Bambara make up the majority of the population and their language is widely spoken and understood. Some other ethnic groups are found in the area, including the Marka and the Fulani. These groups practice both crop cultivation and livestock raising in the same ways as the Bambara, although some of the Fulani are contractual herders. Another group, the Bozo, live along the banks of the Niger river and its tributaries, and practice both farming and fishing. There has been no significant migration into the region, although, in common with the rest of Mali, many people have moved southward and established permanent settlements. There is an increasing shortage of land in the area and the practice of transhumant pastoralism has more or less disappeared.

Three basic crop cultivation zones, arranged concentrically with corresponding land use patterns can be identified in each village. In general the inner village fields in the immediate neighborhood of the settlements are permanently cultivated and manured. The main crops grown on these fields are millet or sorghum intercropped with cowpeas. There is little rotation of crops on these fields. The bush fields constitute the middle zone and are generally sown with intercropped millet and cowpeas, fonio (*Digitaria exilis*) and groundnuts. These fields are rarely supplied with manure, although they are left fallow when possible. Finally, the third and outer zone between adjacent villages is given over to pasture, and may comprise both fallow fields and uncultivated bush. The cropping pattern is dominated by millet, intercropped with cowpeas, followed by sorghum and cowpeas, fonio and groundnuts. The production of groundnuts in this region began during the 1920s, and output increased steadily in the 1950s and 1960s. At this time, the sale of groundnuts constituted the most important source of income for a large number of farmers in the region.

However, when world groundnut prices slumped in the 1970s, and with the discontinuation of the OACV (Opération Arachidière et Culture Vivrière) in 1981, cultivation and output declined rapidly. The parastatal OACV organized the marketing of groundnuts as well as the supply of inputs, furnishing seeds and fertilizer on credit. Low prices, together with the absence of credit facilities and transport at fixed prices, have further discouraged the production of groundnuts in the region, while millet cultivation has subsequently increased.[8]

Eighty percent of the population in the Ségou region make use of in agricultural production systems. The techniques involved have developed considerably since draft animals were introduced in the 1930s. During the 1950s and 1960s constituted an important input in the expansion of groundnut cultivation, and many of the routine tasks were gradually mechanized. Nowadays, many households do not possess draft oxen but cultivate their land using animals and equipment borrowed from other villagers. This entails a considerable delay for some of the poorer households who are forced to wait with tilling and sowing or to carry out only superficial land preparation.

The mechanization of agriculture has resulted in an increase in the total surface area under cultivation, together with a reduction in the length and use of fallow periods. There is also a shortage of land available for cultivation, and it has become impossible to rent and use land from adjacent villages. The expansion of the area cultivated has also had a negative effect on the availability of pastures for grazing animals. Traditionally, animals were released to graze on fallow fields or in the uncultivated bush. However these possibilities have more or less disappeared.

Fertilizer was generally used in the cultivation of groundnuts, but following the fall in prices and given the absence of credit facilities, this practice has now almost ceased. However some of the richer farmers, or those who obtain credit through NGOs, are able to apply some chemical fertilizer to their groundnut, millet and sorghum fields. Animal manure is also utilized, although the quantities are generally insufficient to maintain soil fertility, and the application is concentrated on a limited number of fields.

The number of livestock in the region declined considerably during and after the catastrophic droughts in 1974 and 1984. Although exact estimates of the number of animals lost are not available, the livestock statistics kept by extension services suggest that four times the present number of cattle and twice the present number of small ruminants were to be found in the region before 1974. Livestock management in the area is now exclusively carried out in association with settled farming, and transhumant pastoralism in the sense of large herds passing through the region no longer exists.[9]

Cattle and small ruminants are generally put out to graze on the pasture every day, and are fed with various supplements to differing degrees when they return to the villages. A small number of animals are kept in pens near the houses for intensive fattening. The animals are not sent to graze on pasture land so far away from the village that they cannot return at night. The fodder, notably cowpea haulms, on which the animals are night-fed is usually grown by the farmers themselves. These and other animal feedstuffs fetch ever increasing prices on the rural markets and in Ségou.

Most households keep small ruminants, but few own cattle. In villages where livestock production is being intensified, various possibilities exist for fattening animals and supplementing household incomes. Traditionally, cattle herds are valued as investment resources, but few households are in a position to invest in intensified production given the financial and veterinary obstacles encountered.

The relative importance of different sources of income has changed somewhat over the past twenty years. As mentioned above, groundnuts used to be the main source of cash income, and in conditions of adequate rainfall, cereals production was substantial and stable. As the production of groundnuts declined and as the droughts led to reductions in the number of animals, cutting of wood and migration to other areas became more important as means of securing a livelihood. For those farmers who remained in the agricultural sector and did not become employed in the commercial and handicraft sectors or were unable to maintain their herds and reorientate production strategies towards cereals (given difficulties of access to land), seasonal migration and wood cutting have become important sources of monetary incomes. Approximately one third of the men between the ages of 20 and 35, migrate on a seasonal basis to seek off-farm income.

Following the closing down of the OACV, the extension services in the region have been divided between various projects, organizations and agencies. In the cotton producing zone to the south, the CMDT (Compagnie Malienne du Développement de Textiles) took over the facilities run by the OACV. But in the area investigated, only NGOs and a very limited governmental agricultural and livestock extension service continue to function. Animal vaccination services and the provision of advice in connection with crop cultivation and animal husbandry are almost non-existent.

Traditional systems of social security and reciprocal assistance are still present in the region, although the instability of monetary resources acts as a constraint on the possibility of building on these practices in terms of productive investment. Nevertheless, the system of *Tons villageois* (traditional village associations) through which villagers offer mutual aid and carry out common tasks may form a nucleus for different development activities and credit schemes. These indigenous self-help organizations command considerable support in many villages, notably amongst the Bambara, and in Sakoiba all heads of households are members of the *Ton* which is responsible for the allocation of credit.

Finally, there are three main weekly markets in the region at Ségou, Konodimini and Boussin. All the villages which were studied are within twenty kilometers of one of these markets. Since the cessation of organized groundnut marketing, only very limited quantities of produce are sold outside the region. However, at the Tabaski religious festival, considerable numbers of sheep are traded with buyers from other areas of Mali.

Burkina Faso

Kossi province, in which the villages selected for study are located, is in the western part of Burkina Faso near the border with Mali, to the north-east of the main road from Bobo Dioulasso. This region is characterized by an average annual rainfall of between 800 mm and 1000 mm, and therefore lies within the northern part of the Sudano-Guinean climatic zone. Over the past fifteen years, however, the average annual precipitation in this area has been significantly less, often averaging only around 600 mm.

The landscape is generally flat, sloping gradually to the valley of the Black Volta in the east. The soils are characterized by a high proportion of sand and by their weak retention of organic matter, nitrogen, and phosphates, and the vegetation is generally poor and undiversified. Agricultural production in this area is based on the cultivation of cotton and cereals; both Kouka and Solenzo districts are well known as the heart of the very important cotton growing zone in the west of Burkina Faso.

However, during the drought years in the 1970s and again in the early 1980s, many farmers from the northern Sahelian and central regions of the country moved southward and eastward, often settling this highly productive area. While the livestock owners often arrived in search of pasture and water for their animals, others established themselves through crop cultivation, initially concentrating on cereals but later diversifying into cotton. This influx of migrants continues, as a steady flow of Mossi from the environmentally degraded central plateau of the country find their way to the south and west.

The indigenous population of Bobo and Bwa are now greatly outnumbered by these immigrants, who have rapidly adopted cash crop cultivation. Fulani pastoralists have also settled in this region in considerable numbers, together with people from several other smaller ethnic groups including the Dafing, the Senoufo and the Samogo amongst others. Many of the Fulani in this area arrived around the beginning of the century, and now practice sedentary agriculture, although there are also more recent immigrants in some of the villages, notably Kouka. This cotton-growing area also attracts seasonal laborers from Mali.

High rates of overall population growth have been recorded in several of the villages studied in recent years. There is an enormous variation in size between the villages. The population of Bankouma increased by an annual rate of 17 percent between 1975 and 1985, whereas the population of Selenkoro which has not received any immigrants increased by only 2 percent per year. The distinction between sedentary crop cultivators and livestock- owning pastoralists has become increasingly blurred as the different ethnic groups have settled in the region. But, despite a considerable variation in the production systems and land use patterns between the villages and between the ethnic groups in the region, several main characteristics can be identified.

In all the villages, cotton is grown as the principal cash crop, accounting for between 30 and 45 percent of the total cultivated area. Sorghum is the main cereal crop, though millet is also grown. Maize is becoming increasingly important, particularly in Kouka where over 25 percent of the land is sown to this crop, which is gradually becoming a cash crop for some households. Despite the poor soils, the average yields of these crops are relatively high given the widespread availability of both chemical fertilizers and manure. As far as cotton production is concerned, the role of the parastatal marketing organization SOFITEX (Société des Fibres Textiles) cannot be underestimated. The introduction of cotton in Burkina Faso has been closely linked with the activities of this agency which not only provides credit in connection with the supply of inputs and equipment (such as machinery and tractors), but is also responsible for the collection and marketing of the crop.[10]

Several different production zones can be identified in this region, where environmental factors are significant determinants of the agricultural practices and techniques employed by the farmers. To the east, where Kié and the village of Bankouma are located, heavy soils and readily available water resources present more favorable conditions for intensified agriculture. The villages of Kouka and Kouroumani are located in the central band where the soils are lighter and water is less easily available. The village of Sélenkoro is located in an area where the topography is more uneven and water is in short supply.

Different rates of immigration have been observed in these different zones, but land scarcity is becoming more and more acute throughout the region. Indicators of the extent of land scarcity include the length of the fallow period in the crop rotation, the use of fallow periods by different groups and farmers, the movement of livestock herds in the region, the quality of the land available for newcomers and the length of time over which immigrants have settled and become farmers.

The establishment and the operations of agricultural extension services (including SOFITEX) are significant factors with respect to the adoption of new techniques and technology. Chemical fertilizer is generally applied to fields sown to cotton, although the level of household income is an important determinant of the use of this and other inputs. Some farmers also utilize manure, particularly where the fallow periods have been shortened through the intensification of production. Manure is most frequently used by the Mossi, who also tend to live closer to their fields than the other ethnic groups in the region.

A considerable variation in the patterns of cattle ownership and in the use of animal traction techniques has also been observed in this region, although the official statistics are seriously deficient on these points. Draft animals (oxen) are found in all the villages studied and a steady mechanization of production has also taken place. Draft animals and traction equipment are hired or lent by their owners to the poorer households. The main problem encountered with the animals is a high mortality rate which appears to be related to the lack of good quality fodder crops and adequate veterinary services.

As far as sources of cash income, and differentiation between rich and poor households are concerned, several important factors have been identified. The adoption of improved technology including the mechanization of production using animal traction (and in some cases tractors), and the cultivation of cash crops tend to lead to greater levels of monetary income. Large households also appear to have been able to diversify their sources of income, selling livestock, beer and other products, as well as becoming involved with local commercial and handicraft activities. These households are also in a position to invest in improved techniques and equipment in order to develop both crop cultivation and animal husbandry. However, it is important to note that the possession of animals is traditionally associated with wealth. Furthermore, it appears that long-term residents are generally richer than recent immigrants, particularly in the context of the increasing scarcity of land.

Groupements villageois (village associations) have been established in several villages, where the inhabitants have got together to organize cotton production and marketing in connection with SOFITEX. However these associations do not always function very well despite support from the various extension services and agencies.[11] Finally, as far as marketing is concerned, the infrastructure in the region is relatively well developed although vehicular access to many of the villages is difficult, particularly during the rainy season.

Niger

The six villages studied are situated in the south-west of Niger, two in the district of Niamey and four in Dosso district. Average annual precipitation in this area is about 600 mm, but varies considerably from year to year. The villages of Karakara and Zabori are inhabited mainly by the Haussa, but the latter also has Djerma inhabitants. Tesa and Dokimara are Djerma settlements, whereas Teroudje is almost entirely populated by the Fulani. The village of Birniel Alfari is distinctive in terms of the extent of livestock raising and the large Fulani population. The proximity of the border with Nigeria, and the extensive commercial and cultural links between the two countries, are important factors in the development of this region of Niger.

Land available for grazing animals is becoming increasingly scarce and meager as more and more is taken into use for crop cultivation. The perennial grasses are tending to disappear, and the savannah grasses are being harvested for commercial use. Furthermore, it is estimated that during the last fifteen years the amount of cultivated land has almost doubled, which means that fallow periods have been reduced accordingly. There appear to be several reasons for this, including the high rate of population growth, the declining crop yields which force farmers to extend the cultivated area, the increased agricultural activity of women in the area, and the introduction of animal traction which allows more land to be cultivated.

Tesa is in some ways different from the other villages mentioned above, because the fallow periods are generally a bit longer, but the fields are more unequally divided. Some of the farmers have left the land fallow for more than thirty years, while others abandoned this practice years ago. Birniel Alfari is located close to a fossil river in the Dallol Bosso area, which makes it possible to grow out-of-season crops (*maraîchages de contre saison*). However, millet production in this village is negligible, with just one household growing enough millet to sustain itself. Neither animal traction nor fertilizer has ever been used, but livestock herding ensures the livelihood of the farmers. Given the absence of fallow periods, the land is severely eroded, which again means that lower crop yields are obtained here than in the other villages. Finally, few crops of any commercial value are grown.

Otherwise, the predominant crop is millet which covers 90 percent of the cultivated land in the villages studied. Yields are extremely variable, ranging from 200 kg/ha to 1,200 kg/ha. Official agricultural statistics indicate 566 kg/ha as an average yield, but this seems rather high and the figure is more likely to be around 350 kg/ha. Sorghum is also grown, particularly in areas with heavy soils. Cowpeas are grown alongside millet, which is an attractive option due to the high nutritive value (protein) of this crop and because it can enhance the nitrogen status of the soil. Furthermore, cowpeas are of considerable commercial value and the haulms can be used for fodder.

Sunflower and vouandzou (Bambara groundnut) are also grown, although on a smaller scale. The sunflower crop used to be very important, but as world market prices have gone down, the farmers have found it increasingly difficult to compete in export markets. Nevertheless, some rural development projects (financed by USAID) are being implemented in the region which aim to reintroduce this crop in selected villages. Vouandzou is also, like cowpeas, a crop of high commercial value; in fact it is one of the rare agricultural products which can be sold on the Nigerian market, now that the Naira more or less equates with the CFA franc. This crop is first and foremost cultivated and sold by Haussa women. Finally, the cultivation of cassava is becoming increasingly important, wherever soil and climatic conditions permit, and the production of out-of-season crops is likewise gaining importance, if not markedly so in the villages studied (except in Birniel Alfari, as noted above).

In Tesa, by contrast with the other villages, the women do little work in the fields, except feeding the small ruminants. Agricultural activities are the main sources of income, except in Birniel Alfari. Here, the most important activity, apart from livestock herding, is soda (drink) production, which is, however, in serious trouble, because the price has fallen by two thirds in recent years, partly as a result of the devaluation of the Naira.

In general, traditional agricultural practices with millet and cowpeas as the main crops are going through a severe crisis. Traditional farming techniques are inefficient, and the crop yields are increasingly poor given the unproductive methods of cultivation. The lack of fallow periods is one factor, diminishing precipitation is another (with the happy exception of 1988). But even if weather conditions were to improve, it is doubtful whether this could end the crisis. Studies carried out by ICRISAT conclude that the main limiting factor in Nigerien agriculture is the quality of soil, not the quantity of rain. This leads to the question of what can be done. ICRISAT aims to limit the expansion of the cultivated area, but with the present population boom and increasing mechanization this objective seems rather unrealistic. A return to longer fallow periods seems just as unlikely.[12]

The key problem of maintaining or improving crop productivity per unit area is how to enrich the soil. The use of manure is becoming more common, but this depends on whether farmers have access to carts and other equipment, and in any case, the quantity of animal manure produced per household or village is insufficient in terms of maintaining soil fertility. Crop residues such as leaves and stalks could be used as compost, but then the livestock would have less to eat, and the soil would become even more exposed to wind erosion. Other strategies include legume rotation and leaving the roots in the soil at harvest; also leguminous green mulching, probably a less adoptable option. The devaluation of the Naira in Nigeria means that at least some of the wealthier farmers have started to buy inorganic fertilizer smuggled across the border from Nigeria, which can much increase crop yields depending, on the type and quantity used, timing and placement.[13]

Although the practice of transhumance has been severely hit by the drought, there is extensive livestock raising in the area studied. Some of the wealthier farmers possess immense and rapidly growing herds. But selling livestock on Nigerian markets has more or less been discontinued due both to competition with meat imported from the EC and the devaluation of the Naira. The Fulani are badly affected by this situation, being forced to sell their animals at very low prices. The richer Fulani own herds, but they are obliged to sell off faster than the animals breed. The reason is that grazing land is becoming more scarce, with the result that it is increasingly expensive to feed the animals.

When evaluating the general situation of the region, it is important to remember that this area offers the greatest potential for increasing agricultural productivity in Niger, because it receives more rain than the national average, and because the infrastructure is relatively well developed. For instance, the markets of Niamey and the northern Nigerian towns are within easy reach.

Changing Farming Systems

Variations in the farming systems in the areas studied, and in the socio-economic conditions amongst the households in the sample are considerable. Similarly, the impact of exogenous factors (such as a drought, economic policy reforms, patterns of demand on markets in the region) on the farming systems of the Sahel varies a great deal. One common feature of all the areas studied is that there are no average households, no average years, nor even average periods on which analyses can be based. Changes from one year to the next and differences between one location and another can be dramatic. Nevertheless, although the data collected in the course of this study in order to describe the farming systems and integration of crop and livestock production in the selected villages do not lend themselves to detailed statistical analysis, a number of important trends can be discerned. These are presented in a comparative form in **Table 3.**

A very important ingredient for survival in the Sahelian environment is adaptability. The ability to adapt to new conditions has become an integral part of agricultural production management, but many farmers adopt production strategies which minimize risk in an uncertain natural and economic environment. Given the rapid rate of population growth and the pressure on resources in the region, understanding the ways in which different households and communities overcome production constraints and develop production activities is fundamental to the analysis of integration and changing farming systems.[14]

Table 3. Farming Systems and Integration in the Areas Studied

	Senegal	*Mali*	*Burkina Faso*	*Niger*
Number of villages	6	5	5	6
Total population of villages	5300	4900	13,100	5100[a]
Immigration	Considerable	None	Considerable	Some[b]
Land scarcity	Increasing	Acute	Acute	Increasing[c]
Average crop yields (kg/ha)				
millet/sorghum	500-800[d]	400	1000	350
groundnuts	800-1000	500	600	-
cotton	-	-	1200-1500	-
Fallow periods	Declining	Declining	Very short	Declining
Use of manure	Increasing[e]	Increasing	Increasing[f]	Increasing
Use of fertilizer	Declining	Declining	Widespread	Some[g]
Use of animal traction	Widespread	Borrowing and Hiring	Widespread	Rare
Estimated number of livestock[h]				
cattle	2750	n.a.	5000	2450
horses and donkeys	1450	n.a.	500	n.a.
small ruminants	5350	n.a.	n.a.	n.a.
Transhumance	Declining	Disappeared	Rare	Declining

a. Plus the village of Zabori, for which population data were unavailable
b. From drought affected northern regions
c. Considerable variation between the villages
d. Improved varieties with higher yields also used
e. Not applied on groundnut crop
f. Notably by immigrants
g. Some smuggled across the border from Nigeria
h. Figures based on estimates by veterinary services
Source: Country studies

The focal points of this study concerned the allocation of resources, particularly land, between different crop and livestock production activities, the adoption of techniques such as animal traction, the use of manure and crop residues, and the patterns of income generation and distribution in the households and rural communities. The diversity between households arising from the ownership of different assets such as land, labor, livestock, and farm equipment can be explained in terms of various historical, environmental and economic factors. However, there are clearly "rich" and "poor" villages in the areas studied. A number of factors were identified to explain such differences in the context of changing farming techniques and systems. These are further examined in the next chapter.

3. *Agricultural Production in the Economic and Socio-Cultural Context*

The Economic Environment

Changes in crop and animal production systems in the Sahel over the past twenty to thirty years have taken place in an increasingly difficult economic context, characterized by low growth rates in agricultural and industrial production relative to very low levels of per capita GNP. On the other hand, the parastatal and public service sectors have grown rapidly, fueling an increasing demand for imports of energy, foodstuffs, and both consumer and capital goods. However, exports of agricultural products (as well as those from the mining and manufacturing sectors) have also grown very slowly, and trade deficits have steadily increased. Despite the considerable flows of foreign aid to the region, debt burdens accumulated towards the beginning of the 1980s, while balance of payments deficits became acute (OECD, 1988).

Structural Adjustment, Prices, and Marketing

The structural adjustment programs which were introduced in the majority of West African countries during the 1980s, sought to reverse the deteriorating economic conditions of these countries, notably in terms of balance of payments and government budgetary deficits, through measures designed to change the structure of production and to produce tradeable goods in greater quantities. Attention generally focused on efforts to improve agricultural output and growth, where production incentives in the form of price policies assumed considerable significance.[15]

Price reforms in structural adjustment programs emphasized the removal of subsidies and the reduction of the taxation on agriculture, by adjusting exchange rates and by bringing domestic producer prices into line with international prices. At the same time, reducing the role of the public sector, in order to cut the high costs of government intervention in agricultural marketing, was another major objective. These liberalization and privatization policies, and other measures introduced through structural adjustment programs, aimed to increase producer prices and to promote the involvement of the private sector in agricultural marketing, strategies conceived as essential prerequisites for stimulating supply responses and thereby increasing agricultural output.

However, it appears that the economic policies pursued by the governments of Senegal, Mali and Niger during the 1980s imposed rather austere conditions on the agricultural sector. The withdrawal of parastatal agencies from much of the agricultural sector generally resulted in increases in farmgate prices of inputs and made the acquisition of equipment and draft animals more difficult, due to the cessation of credit schemes. These increases in costs were not compensated by increases in the prices of crops and livestock. Furthermore, public expenditure cuts resulted in the closure of many of the extension service programs which had previously operated in the areas.[16]

The 1980s were also marked by fluctuations and a general deterioration in the terms of trade of agricultural products on international markets. These changing price relationships in the Sahel had a severe negative impact on farm incomes in all the areas studied. Declining world market prices for groundnuts and cotton, the two main cash crops, were passed on to the farmers. In Senegal, groundnut producer prices fell 21 percent in real terms between 1981-82 and 1987-88. In 1988-89 the producer price was further reduced to 70 CFAF/kg, a drop of 20 CFAF/kg from the previous year. This decline was responsible for a major reduction in farm incomes. However the fall in the price of cotton in Burkina Faso during this period was much less. Furthermore, the CFA franc was overvalued in all four countries, leading to unfavorable terms of trade between the rural and urban sectors, which further encouraged farmers to increase their income through non-farm activities.

The grain marketing environment in the Sahelian countries is weak, characterized by poor infrastructure, small quantities traded, inadequate local storage and poor market information. In 1987 and 1988, the post-harvest prices of millet and sorghum declined substantially in real terms. There are also major seasonal price variations which reflect the poor marketing situation, and prices prior to the following harvest may rise by as much as 100 percent, as observed in the villages studied in Mali and Niger.[17] The liberalization of cereals marketing in connection with adjustment programs has not resulted in any significant increases in producer prices. Indeed, given the considerable improvement in rainfall levels after 1985, record harvests were recorded throughout the Sahel and prices dropped accordingly.[18]

Low cereal prices are a significant disincentive to on-farm investment. Meanwhile the prices of most inputs have risen substantially. As noted above, the abolition of state- run credit organizations and subsidies, and the privatization of input delivery systems have led to big price rises for fertilizers, chemicals, and agricultural equipment because the previous parastatal agencies were heavily subsidized. This has greatly reduced fertilizer and equipment purchases on all farms in the areas studied, except for those by the richer cotton farmers in Burkina Faso.

Livestock prices are largely determined by supply and demand. These fluctuate around cycles of drought and recovery from drought, with very low prices prevailing during drought periods as livestock owners sell off their stock. However, imports of frozen meat to the main coastal markets have increased substantially during the past five years. A large proportion of such imports were in the form of subsidized meat imports from the EC. In 1986, the EC exported 39,437 ton to Côte d'Ivoire, Togo and Benin out of total imports into these countries of just over 40,000 ton. Furthermore, the price of subsidized EC beef (cif) was about half the prevailing world beef price.[19]

The arrival of large quantities of subsidized meat has had a severe negative impact on livestock prices in the Sahel which have been stagnant in current values and declined in real terms during the second half of the 1980s. In addition, imports of milk, totalling about 30,000 ton per annum between 1984 and 1986 to the four countries studied, some in the form of food aid, have also acted as a disincentive for domestic milk production.[20] Recent trade and marketing policy analysis in West Africa has focused on the need to improve transport systems and reduce transaction costs in order to enable Sahelian producers to maximize the benefits from animal product sales in the coastal countries.

Agricultural Incomes

The poor price environment is reflected in low and declining farm incomes. As shown in **Table 4**, analyses of returns to land and labor for the principal crops grown in the villages studied revealed very low returns to family labor, below 400 CFAF per day for all crops except cotton. Returns to land were also very low, in the range 11,000 to 23,000 CFAF per hectare for millet, or millet intercropped with cowpeas and groundnuts, in Senegal, Mali and Niger. Returns to land for sorghum in Burkina Faso were higher at 28,000 CFAF, and only cotton provided a satisfactory return of 52,000 CFAF.

Only farmers growing cash crops of groundnuts or cotton obtained a cash income. In Senegal there were wide variations in groundnut revenue according to area planted. The average income per household from groundnuts was 98,000 CFAF but in four of the villages studied, with a much smaller cultivated area, groundnut revenue was only 38,000 CFAF. However, although the cotton farmers in Burkina Faso cultivated smaller areas, they earned cash incomes of 146,000 CFAF on average. But it is also important to reiterate that these estimates of average household incomes mask considerable variations; a discussion of the factors which influence income distribution, within and between the villages studied is outlined below.

Only one village in the area studied, Boussin in Mali, earned a significant cash income from the sale of millet, given the very large area cultivated. Furthermore, the production of cereals for subsistence requirements by many households in the villages studied was insufficient. Out of the total sample of twenty-two villages most of the households in fifteen of them did not produce sufficient cereals. In aggregate terms, all of the villages in Niger, and most in Senegal and Mali, were in deficit.

Table 4. Crop Production Budgets and Returns to Land and Labor

	Revenue (CFA/ha)	*Input costs (CFA/ha)*[a]	*Number of mandays*	*Returns per ha. (CFA)*	*Returns per manday (CFA)*
Senegal					
groundnuts	48,500	35,960	36.5	12,540	340
millet	25,000	13,700	39	11,300	290
Mali					
millet intercropped with cowpeas	36,000	19,600	63	16,400	260
Burkina Faso					
cotton	125,400	73,400	105	52,000	500
sorghum	48,000	19,700	87	28,300	330
Niger					
millet intercropped with cowpeas	32,000	8,680	64	23,320	360

a. Including, where applicable, costs of hired labor, seed, fertilizer, and equipment

Source: Study reports

Incomes from livestock are very volatile, and depend heavily on pasture availability, fodder prices and, livestock mortality levels. It was estimated that the average annual income from one large ruminant was about 8,000 to 9,000 CFAF while that from one small ruminant was between 1,500 and 3,000 CFAF. In terms of annual returns per TLU, small ruminant raising is more profitable. It is important to note, however, that a significant supplementary income is obtained by some crop farmers from the sale of crop residues produced in excess of their livestock requirements.

Population and Resources

Many of the villages studied have registered very rapid population growth rates due to the substantial immigration which has compounded already high natural growth rates. The total population of the four countries studied, together with projections and estimates of the numbers of inhabitants in the years 2000 and 2025 are presented in **Table 5**.

In Senegal, all villages received large numbers of migrants during the groundnut boom in the 1970s, and some are still receiving immigrants either from areas with even more acute land shortage or from the north as a result of drought. Almost all land is now occupied and cultivated. In the villages studied in Mali no new settlers have arrived since the early 1970s, and all land and that in the neighboring villages is now fully occupied.

The immigration of the Mossi to the villages studied in Burkina Faso has been dramatic, completely changing the ethnic composition of many villages. One village, Bankouma, had an average annual population growth rate of 16.8 percent between 1975 and 1985. In three of the villages studied, the Mossi are the dominant ethnic group. The rapid growth of population has, within a relatively short space of time, turned an area with abundant land to one of chronic shortage. Conflicts over access to land both between crop farmers and between farmers and pastoralists have become more frequent and serious. The villages studied in Niger have also received immigrants who mostly come from further north as a result of the drought. In Niger most village land was also fully utilized and in some villages there was an acute land shortage.

The high rates of growth of the human population and increases in the numbers of livestock in the Sahel (following the drought in early 1980s) have greatly augmented the pressure on available land resources. This has contributed to declining fallow periods and soil fertility with consequent lower yields. Pasture production has declined due to drought, overstocking, deforestation, and burning. Furthermore, as noted earlier, not only has the quantity of rainfall recorded in the Sahel since the 1960s decreased, but its temporal variability has

Table 5. Population and Growth Projections

	Total population in 1987 (millions)	*Average annual growth rate estimates (1987-2000)*	*Projected population (millions)*	
			2000	*2025*
Senegal	7	3.1%	10	20
Mali	8	3.0%	11	24
Burkina Faso	8	2.9%	12	23
Niger	7	3.2%	10	22

Source: World Bank, World Development Report, 1989

increased. Recurrent drought and the apparent trend towards greater aridity in the region, exacerbated by increased water runoff from degraded and eroded land surfaces, has reduced the recharge of aquifers. Given the increased demand for water by the growing population, the level of the water tables appears to be falling, with serious consequences for their users.[21]

Agricultural Production and Socio-Cultural Organization

A number of interesting apparent paradoxes were identified during the course of the study. Data collected from the household surveys and discussions with villagers indicated that:

- Although it appears that both crop and livestock production in Senegal, Mali and Niger are not very remunerative occupations, nevertheless, a large number of households in Senegal and Mali maintain animal traction, which seems to be financially unjustifiable.

- Constraints affecting all the households in the areas studied include drought and other adverse weather conditions, as well as structural adjustment policies pursued by governments. Notwithstanding the necessity to undertake economic policy reforms, these programs have resulted in increased input costs and reduced extension service and credit facilities, which have not been compensated for by increases in the prices of crops and livestock. Nevertheless, some households appear not only to have overcome these constraints, but also actually to thrive on them, becoming considerably better off than before.

- Because of established land rights, land scarcity problems are more acute for pastoralists than for farmers, and more serious for immigrants than for indigenous inhabitants. However, the studies in Burkina Faso show that this generalization does not apply to the major immigrant group, the Mossi, for they do not suffer most from scarcity of land, whereas those who settled earlier are having an increasingly hard time.

There are, however, certain elements in the social system which can help in understanding these issues and shed some light on the organization of rural communities. The socio-cultural relations in the rural communities in question are basically formed by a web of relationships including domination, submission, authority, obedience, instruction, learning, the rendering of services and counter-services, and mutual dependence all of which amount to a socio-cultural set of ethics and a sense of belonging, either to a kinship unit or to an ethnic group.

Homogeneous and Heterogeneous Social Organization

The kinship and ethnic systems of the Sahel are complex and vary considerably from one area to another. An understanding of these social and cultural factors is important in the search for explanations of strategies which may contribute to increasing incomes and improving agricultural production systems.[22] Hence knowledge of how farmers obtain labor, agricultural equipment, draft animals, credit, and land is essential.

As noted structural adjustment programs which reduced subsidies in Senegal, Mali and Niger led to a decline in the use of key inputs such as fertilizer and improved seeds, while the lack of extension services led to rather unskilled use of these inputs where they are still employed. Furthermore, with no public sector or subsidized sale, the working stock of equipment such as harrows and ploughs is getting older. In the wake of these measures markets in second-hand agricultural equipment flourish.

With virtually no public credit schemes to facilitate the purchase of equipment, animals or other inputs, farmers turn to each other to obtain the different inputs. Socio-cultural factors play a key role in the distribution of these inputs. The items exchanged among households vary a great deal. Sometimes poorer households need to borrow oxen or equipment and repay in labor or in cash. Sometimes they need cash to buy food in order to avoid selling equipment and will repay through labor.

Generally, such exchanges are kept within ethnic or more often kinship group even if they involve cash payment. In this respect, the historical background of the villages studied in Senegal, Mali and Niger suggests that it is possible to divide them into two broad categories:

a. Villages which were founded by one person, frequently several generations ago and the majority of the inhabitants consider themselves to be the founder's descendants. Here the social system appears to be very homogeneous. These villages are characterized by substantial exchanges of favors and goods amongst the households, following the customary practices of the ethnic group. Many communal activities, such as the collection of money for village projects including well digging or tree planting are encountered, and there is often a high rate of participation in local soil conservation projects. The homogeneity and the social cohesion in these villages do not indicate an egalitarian structure or a social system free of conflicts, but they denote a well-established and accepted structure of power, and a set of social rules.

b. Villages which, because of favorable water resources, grazing areas, or land availability, have attracted many settlers. When neighboring regions suffered from natural calamities, a substantial number of farmers were forced to migrate. The inflow of migrants has often resulted in a situation where the immigrants outnumber the descendants of the founder of the village thus creating a very heterogeneous village. In contrast to the situation found in the homogeneous villages, communal activities appear to fail due to the general suspicion and animosity among inhabitants of these heterogeneous villages. No one contributes to village funds and participation in local NGO projects does not last long. The exchange of favors and goods among different households is limited to the very closest relatives and nobody expects to get any help from other villagers in times of trouble.

Quarrels over land are among the most frequently observed reasons for animosity in the villages. Since land rights are generally established according to two parallel codes, the traditional and the formal legal code, there is a considerable risk of conflicts arising. In the homogeneous villages, the same persons assume both traditional authority and occupy seats on the village council which deals with disputes about land on a formal legal basis, and there are no open conflicts. However, in the heterogeneous villages, newly settled farmers rarely obtain permanent rights over land through the traditional code and therefore invoke their legal rights to land. Frequently, the traditional leaders head the village council, but their authority is often not recognized, and if there are many new settlers disputes over the legitimacy of their power often result in open conflicts.

Social Cohesion and Differentiation

An interesting picture emerges from a comparison of the situation of the households studied in 1988 with that prevailing at the beginning of the 1980s. Generally, the homogeneous villages have experienced an increased social and economic stratification, whereas the heterogeneous villages have experienced a reduced social differentiation. At the same time, while the poorest group in the heterogeneous villages has become more impoverished, there appears to be a lower limit as to how poor the poorest group in the homogeneous villages can become. A number of different reasons for these tendencies were identified in the course of the study.

Social cohesion in the homogeneous villages provides a safety net for the poorest group in the village; the richer households assist the poorer households when needed, thus preventing them from having to sell equipment or draft animals. In the heterogeneous villages, on the other hand, no safety net exists to help the unfortunate in times of crises. This explains why some households in the homogeneous villages who appeared to be in the same situation as the poor households in the heterogeneous villages at the beginning of the 1980s, have managed to maintain their production.

Providing a safety net and occasionally offering assistance does not prevent the wealthier households from expanding their cultivated areas. The exchange between the wealthier and the poorer households includes mechanisms whereby members of the poorer households work for their patrons. A poor household's need for help when affected by a crisis can be so desperate that the importance of close relationships between themselves and their richer relatives forces them to assist their wealthier relatives as often as they can.

In a number of poor, homogeneous villages in the poorer regions of Mali and Niger, poverty is much more acute than in Senegal, and wealthier kin have not been able to help poorer kin to maintain or procure animal traction, having enough trouble to sustain themselves as it is. The safety net then consists of providing food, or money to buy food during the hungry season or to rent equipment.[23]

The price to be paid for this kind of safety net may appear rather insignificant, but the ability to control the timing of labor services is the key element. This control enables the patron to cultivate his own fields before lending or hiring his equipment to his dependents. In the poorer villages in Mali and Niger, however, income from the hiring of equipment exceeds the potential income from cultivating an extra hectare, and is more reliable. Households with a full range of traction equipment often choose to hire out the equipment and the draft animals to fellow villagers when the area required for food production has been tilled. The same control also enables the patron to call his dependents for weeding precisely when needed, and not when it is most convenient for his dependents; both would hardly be possible since both have fields to weed at the same time.

It was difficult to quantify the labor, equipment, and amounts of food exchanged, but it appears that where one of the parties is in a desperate situation and thus willing to pay a high price for the exchange, the control over timing is crucial. The patron can thus offer his services at a time when they were otherwise of little value to himself, while he can demand his dependents' return services at the time when the dependents can least afford them. Since these relations are kept mainly within kinship boundaries, where the social sanctions for the non-fulfillment of obligations include a serious loss of prestige as well as a possible loss of the option for future exchanges, they serve to reinforce social cohesion and to fortify the existing power structure.

Membership of an extended social system offers a safety net for the poor, and an important potential for exploitation for the wealthy. This is a very important asset for the wealthier farmers in the homogeneous villages, unavailable to those in the heterogeneous villages. This may be even more pronounced when general farming conditions are adverse, as they have been recently. The wealthier farmers in the heterogeneous villages do not have any extra manpower to call upon and are therefore not cushioned against crises. The richer farmers in the homogeneous villages on the other hand, have the possibility of taking on an extensive labor force, and in a crisis the poorer dependents will be very anxious to demonstrate the close ties of mutual assistance.[24]

Animal Traction

As far as animal traction is concerned, the socio-cultural relations in the socially homogeneous villages give rise to a peculiar situation. In the wealthier villages, this set of relations enables the poorer farmers to maintain animal traction even though their economic situation does not justify this practice, and purchase of equipment would be out of the question without external assistance. In the poor villages on the other hand, the richest farmers are often not better off than the poorer farmers in the wealthier villages, but they are able to obtain animal traction through exchanges with the poorest farmers in the village. Hiring out the equipment for cash provides the owners with a sufficient economic rationale for maintaining animal traction in spite of low crop prices.

The socio-cultural relations thus contribute to some extent to maintaining the use of draft power which would otherwise have been eradicated in periods of crisis. Communities characterized by social cohesion manage to cope with unremunerative crop prices to a degree which far exceeds the point at which communities of a heterogeneous character would abandon animal traction. This occurs as a result of the exchanges which seem to function more smoothly and more extensively in homogeneous than in heterogeneous villages.

On the other hand, social coherence alone does not carry much weight if the general economic conditions do not leave any margin for surplus extraction, as in the case of the villages studied in Niger. Very few farmers in this example can pay anything in return for labor (not even through the social safety net) and therefore it appears that very few farmers profit from social coherence. A strong system of coherence is thus not a guarantee for the maintenance of animal traction or any other form of integration between livestock raising and crop cultivation. However, crop prices do not necessarily have to be so high that they alone can sustain mechanized farming, if strong social coherence is found in the community. This suggests that social coherence provides a cushion and a considerable time-lag against the impact of economic adversity, and also that the general trend could be towards a demechanization of farming systems if no intervention takes place.[25]

Once it has been established that socio-cultural relations can ensure that animal traction is maintained (or at least discontinuation of this practice delayed), the difference between maintaining and adopting animal traction has to be borne in mind. While the system of socio-cultural relations ensures the feasibility of maintaining animal traction even though crop prices fall, increasing land scarcity and the abolition of credit and extension services tend to make animal traction less profitable for the individual farmer. However, socio-cultural network does not seem to enable farmers without animal traction to adopt such practices if the conditions of crop prices, land, credit, and extension are adverse. Moreover, it seems that a favorable combination of all four factors is needed to ensure the adoption of mixed farming and especially animal traction. In Burkina Faso for example, good crop prices and land availability alone do not assure the adoption of animal traction, but with the provision of extension and credit services, animal traction is adopted.

Labor and Credit

One type of labor organization seems to be disappearing in some places. In the past, working parties of local men, women or young people were quite common in many villages. They could be called upon by all villagers to carry out very arduous tasks, such as weeding and harvesting. In many ways, this institution ensured that poorer households, faced with insufficient labor due to illness or death in the family, could still harvest their crops.

The working parties still exist, but their character has changed. In the areas studied in Senegal and Burkina Faso, working parties are now mainly found working the land of the wealthier villagers, and the symbolic meal given to the laborers is now supplemented or altogether replaced by either money or access to draft animals and equipment. The labor "price increase" is mainly made possible by the presence of animal traction equipment, and the poorer farmers have changed from buying it to selling it in order to survive.

In Niger, working parties are also encountered, but their importance is diminishing since farmers feel that it is humiliating to ask neighbors to give up a day to work for them. In Mali, on the other hand, working parties of young men are fairly common. The indigenous village association (*Ton Villageois*) which includes all heads of households in a village can be approached for assistance, and it will then order the working party to assist the petitioner. To the young men, the performance of the duties through the *Ton* forms a rite of passage which ensures their future right to call for assistance. The generally higher levels of cash revenue in Senegal and in Burkina Faso have contributed to the decrease in the number of working parties compared with Mali.

The picture is very much the same when it comes to credit. It is possible to borrow money from a money lender, but at extortionate interest rates which rise markedly during the *soudure*. If, however, the farmer belongs to a social majority, the social sanctions against default are so vigorous that the lender runs less risk and thus charges less.

This social mechanism is being exploited in connection with a development project in Mali. The external aid agency provides credit for inputs, equipment, and oxen, but all requests for credit have to be accepted and supported by the *Ton*. If a farmer fails to repay, the entire *Ton* is obliged to reimburse his debts. It is still too early to judge the success and impact of this scheme since it has only operated for a few years, but so far the agency concerned has not experienced any serious defaults.

Land, Settlement, and Scarcity

Access to land is generally decided by the *Chef de Village* and the male descendants of the original village founder as the traditional forum, and by a legally constituted village council. **Land cannot be bought or sold**; access to land for adult sons comes through the death of their father or through his allocation of pieces of land for their private use. For new settlers, on the other hand, petitions for land through the traditional structures do not generally give permanent usufruct rights to land but require a renewed petition every year. At this point, conflicts often arise when settlers invoke their formal legal rights to the land they cultivate, but they rarely succeed in getting permanent land rights. Thus settlers face serious constraints and potential ostracism.

It is therefore notable that in Burkina Faso, the settlement of the Mossi has not generally placed them in the most vulnerable social and economic positions. Here, a procedure is usually followed whereby already settled immigrants act as intermediaries between the *Chef de Village*, the local authority controlling the allocation of land, and the new settler. Often, new settlers choose a village where relatives can vouch for them, and this results in the establishment of real kinship ties between the two farmers, which can evolve into actual kinship through the intermarriage of their children. Hence, although they are immigrants, the Mossi community often forms a solid social structure of its own.

In many villages, the Mossi make up more than 50 percent of the population, and these villages include two parallel, fairly homogeneous large social structures: that of the Bobo, the original inhabitants, and that of the Mossi, the major immigrant group. There is also a third group, however, made up of families who settled twenty-five or more years ago, but they constitute only a small fraction of the population. These households of the Dafing, Samogo, Bambara, Kado, Senofo and to some extent the Fulani have not been resident in the area for centuries as have the Bobo, nor do they form 50 percent or more of the population, as do the Mossi. Whereas the Mossi have left the central plateau mainly because of drought and land degradation and often arrived in huge waves, the other settler groups have not come from areas of extensive environmental degradation, and have thus made their way in much smaller numbers and over a long period of time.

Social and economic organization in these villages is in many ways segregated and kept within ethnic boundaries. With serious implications for the smaller immigrant communities. Being a minority reduces its ability to create effective social safety nets, and also results in potential exploitation. More significant from a land access point of view, are the local political implications. The Bobo maintain certain prerogatives due to their seniority in the area. By outnumbering the other ethnic groups the Mossi have created a significant power base through which they are able to influence the village cooperatives, and to exert a heavy influence on the distribution of land. This has led to the marginalization of the smaller ethnic groups which find it increasingly difficult to obtain satisfaction from renewed petitions for land. In a number of villages, the massive inflow of immigrants has led to some emigration (although not to the same extent) by farmers belonging to those ethnic minorities which have suffered from social and economic ostracism.

This migration phenomenon is instructive in several ways. The vulnerable group is made up of immigrants, and even a relatively long history in the area does not entitle settlers to the land they cultivate. On the other hand, this disadvantage is offset by the numbers of immigrants, their social cohesion and their "political presence" in the village. The system of mutual vouching for new settlers and the use of intermediaries when petitioning for land makes it very difficult to reject requests from the large Mossi community. The previously settled but weaker farmers suffer from the Bobo agreeing to requests for land from the Mossi.

Allocation of Resources

The unequal distribution of production factors among farmers has led to different ways of exploiting these factors. Basically, two patterns can be observed when looking at the ways in which farmers allocate land, time and capital to different crops and activities. The wealthier farmers allocate land to staple food crops in order to secure their households' own consumption, and after that, land is allocated to the cash crop in proportion to the households' assets of traction equipment and labor power. This gives a rather balanced use of resources and indicates a certain mastery of events by the farmer. The poorer farmers strive to do the same, but due to the lack of equipment, animals, ready cash for seeds, or manpower, the proportion of the area which they allocate to cash crops is much smaller than it is for the wealthy farmers and varies from year to year.

In Senegal, wealthy farmers allocate more land to groundnuts than do the poorer farmers; in Burkina Faso the main crop is cotton and in Mali it is millet. In Mali many households are deficient in cereals and have no capital with which to increase their production, and this enables the wealthy farmers to sell staple crops at a profit. But in Senegal and in Mali, given the prevailing market prices, the profits from the production of cash crops (groundnuts or millet) have reached an upper limit. Farmers do not use their profits to transform their production system by buying tractors like the cotton farmers in Burkina Faso. Instead, capital is invested partly in the traditional "bank" (animals), but also in lucrative off-farm businesses such as money lending, public transport, commercial activities and hiring of equipment.

Farmers who cannot produce the households' requirements for staple crops try to bridge the gap by turning to off-farm activities. However, lacking the financial resources enabling them to undertake activities with high entry costs, they resort to illegal wood-cutting, seasonal migration, and farmhand jobs in the area. Such occupations offer far lower potential gains than transport and commerce.

Many of the farmers who may be classified as being between these two groups by maintaining animal traction, but with no surplus to invest in transport or commerce, basically follow the pattern of land allocation of the wealthy farmers. What distinguishes them from this latter group is that they are highly dependent on social relations, either through wealthier relatives who have helped them in times of need, or through poorer relatives to whom they hired their equipment. Hence, they spend substantial amounts of time on the maintenance of these social relationships, either when they are actually working for a patron, or when they are without their own equipment, thus reducing their own potential for cultivating the land.

Horse traction in Senegal

"Night parking"

4. *Integration - Trends and Issues*

The Process of Integration

There are two main factors behind the gradual evolution from separate crop and livestock production systems interacting with each other to integrated mixed farming systems. These are population growth and the introduction and promotion of cash crops. Both contribute to an increase in the cultivated area at the expense of pastoral grazing areas. Declining average annual rainfall accentuated by periodic drought has also adversely affected the capability of large areas of the Sahel to support both human and livestock populations, and has increased the pressure on land resources. Furthermore, the introduction of cash crops, particularly groundnuts and cotton in Senegal, Mali, and Burkina Faso, has acted as an incentive to expand the area cultivated. The use of draft animals has further accelerated the process of agricultural expansion, but even without the introduction of these techniques the same increase in cultivated areas would probably have taken place, but over a longer period of time.

Thus it appears that the process of integrating livestock into crop production systems is initiated when cultivable land becomes scarce in relation to population. Instead of two independent complementary production systems interacting through the exchange of by-products and factors of production, there is now competition for the key production factor, land. As land becomes ever more scarce the by-products of the two systems, crop residues and manure, become increasingly valuable, the former for feed and the latter for fertilization.

Crop farmers require increasing quantities of manure to fertilize fields the fertility of which is declining due to increased cropping intensity and reduced fallow periods. The reduction or elimination of fallow periods results in falling crop yields unless ever more fertilizer or manure is applied. In order to obtain more manure the farmers require more livestock for which they need more crop residues, and so on.

Meanwhile, pastoralists, faced with a reduction in the pasture area as the best grazing land is brought under cultivation, become more dependent on crop residues which assume a progressively greater share of the total feed. But as crop residues become more valuable, crop farmers will use them for their own livestock and the residues will no longer be available as feed for the animals belonging to the pastoralists. Thus as land pressure increases there is an incentive for pastoralists to settle and become arable farmers themselves, producing crop residues for animal feed and cereals for domestic consumption, thereby becoming less dependent on the previously settled crop farmers.

In the evolution from extensive to intensive production systems, manure and crop residues rise in value not only on account of their increasing importance for keeping their animals alive and maintaining soil fertility, but also because of the rising demand (through population growth) for the end products, namely cereals, meat and milk. Farmers are in effect maximizing the efficient use of both by-products. Crop residues are transported to households where they are fed to livestock maintained there during all or part of the dry season, instead of being left on the fields where they may be consumed by other people's stock, or by termites. But the residual value of these products as soil fertilizer is extremely small after being burnt with consequent loss of nitrogen and organic matter. In order to increase the supply of manure, crop farmers establish night paddocks and maintain more livestock at the household for longer periods. A number of additional factors reinforce these processes:

- Herding costs are rising steadily, in terms of the remuneration in cash and in kind (milk or animals) paid to herders. With declining incomes from crop cultivation (except in the cash crop zone in Burkina Faso), fewer farmers can afford such costs. The trend towards increased crop cultivation implies that stock numbers per herder during the cropping season must be reduced.

- Mortality levels are believed to be rising due both to undernutrition and ineffective veterinary services. Distances between pastures and water points become ever greater in the dry season and the animals become progressively weaker from insufficient food. Where feed and water can be provided to the livestock maintained at the household during the dry season, the feed requirement will be less because less energy is expended, and weight losses and mortality rates will be lower.

- Herders often combine both their own stock and those entrusted to them by the crop farmers. But in the face of limited grazing opportunities and access to water, preferential treatment may be given to their own animals, which gives rise to an underlying element of distrust between livestock owners and the herders. When a crop farmer's animal dies, the explanations offered by the herders are rarely accepted at face value.

- The maintenance of livestock at the household enables the owner to keep them under constant surveillance. Feeding and watering can be done by the owner's family, usually women and children, whose labor has a low opportunity cost during the dry season.

- The relatively recent practices of collecting, transporting, and storing straw and dried grass from the pastures (for "zero-grazing") in order to compensate for shortages of crop residues, have reduced the quality of pasture for both transhumant and village herds reinforcing the trend towards stock maintenance at the household. By implicitly placing an economic value on bush straw, burning is discouraged with attendant and important environmental benefits. But pastoralists may lose access to this grass unless they can negotiate shares.

On the other hand, intensified and integrated crop and animal production systems (at the household) involve considerable labor inputs both in collecting feed and in transporting manure to the fields. These are usually carried out during the dry season when the opportunity cost of labor is lower. There may also be some health risks involved in maintaining larger herds at the household.

The use of draft animals is not the only, or the key, issue in the development of integrated farming systems in the Sahel. But the introduction of draft animals has accelerated the process of integration through their impact on land use patterns. The economic justification for the introduction of draft animals stemmed from the low price of land in relation to labor. The main growth in animal traction occurred between the 1950s and 1970s especially in Senegal and Mali, when land was relatively abundant but rural labor costs were rising under the influence of rising urban incomes (linked to expanded employment opportunities). Cash crop production further encouraged the acquisition of draft animals and equipment, since money was available to finance such purchases. The introduction of draft animals in connection with carts has also increased the opportunities to earn non-farm incomes by using the animals and carts in the transport sector to carry a variety of goods, such as wood, water, building materials, and so on.

Ploughing with oxen

Integration in the Areas Studied

The process of integration is well established in the areas studied and most farmers feed crop residues to their livestock and spread manure on their fields. An increasing number of stock, including horses, donkeys, oxen, and cows, as well as small ruminants are kept near the households for part or all of the year in all of the villages.

Manure Use

The trend towards keeping livestock at the households clearly results in an increase in the quantity of manure deposited there or in night paddocks. As manuring of fields by transhumant herds diminishes, the value of manure collected from such night paddocks rises. Being a bulky commodity manure is not yet traded in the markets of the villages. The transport and spreading of manure is labor intensive and can most effectively be undertaken using a cart. Most farmers in the villages use donkeys (or horses in Senegal) and carts although a few cases of head transport were noted in Niger.[26]

Eighty-two percent of the households included in the survey in **Senegal** transported manure to the fields, the manure coming principally from horses and small ruminants. Shortage of animals was the main reason for not transporting manure. Meanwhile it appears that "parking" of herds on fields is declining both as a result of declining numbers of livestock and fewer transhumant herds. The growth in manure application has accompanied the decline in fallowing, and 34 percent of the households reported no fallow periods in the crop rotation.

It was difficult to estimate the quantities applied, but they were mostly in the range of 500 kg to 1,700 kg per hectare. Manure was applied only to the millet crop, since manure use on groundnuts was thought to cause excessive leaf growth and reduced nut yields. In Senegal only, manure deposited on fields from night parking is burnt before the cultivation of the next crop. This practice is justified by the farmers as necessary to allow the smooth passage of the equipment, in particular the planter. Much of the value of the manure is lost through nitrogen gas emission during burning and the ash being scattered in the wind.

There are no transhumant herds in the villages studied in **Mali** and the transport and spreading of manure is more widely practiced than in the other countries. Forty households (70 percent of the sample) transported manure from cattle (and oxen) and fifty-three households (93 percent) transported small ruminant manure. The quantities transported were not specified but the Agricultural Research Station at N'Tala estimates that 300 kg of dry matter per TLU are available each year. Efforts to promote composting of manure as part of the OACV groundnut scheme were unsuccessful due to the high opportunity cost of labor.

Out of the sixty-three households surveyed in **Burkina Faso**, only twenty transported manure to their fields. Of those who did not, the principal reasons advanced were shortage of carts or donkeys and lack of time. Many indigenous residents still had sufficient fallow land and did not use manure. The main initiators of manure use were the immigrant Mossi and this practice is also now vigorously promoted by the extension service. The practice of night parking on fields by transhumant herds is declining since many former transhumant pastoralists have settled and use their herds to manure their own fields.

In **Niger** the practices of manure transport and spreading were more widespread with forty-six out of fifty-four households in three of the villages studied using these techniques. These households also indicated that they were increasing the quantities transported. The supply of manure from transhumant herds was on the decline, but the quantities transported from the households were not sufficient in terms of soil fertility improvement to compensate for this loss.

Collection of Crop Residues

The collection of crop residues from fields sown with millet, sorghum, groundnuts, cowpeas and pigeon peas is steadily increasing as a larger proportion of the livestock is maintained at the household. Furthermore, the development of fodder markets both in towns and in villages is growing. In addition to the collection of crop residues, farmers also collect straw from the natural pastures. The crop residues are usually stored on top of barns ("hangers") where they are protected from termites; but here they are exposed to the sun and thus lose some of their nutritive value. There was no evidence of households using sorghum or millet stalks as fuel. Where left on the field, sorghum and millet stover is burnt before preparing the land for the next crop. All groundnut and cowpea haulms are collected, since these have significantly higher nutritive values than cereal stover.[27]

In **Senegal**, groundnut haulms are all transported to the household for feeding to horses, oxen, donkeys and small ruminants. In addition, farmers without adequate groundnut haulms collect bush straw. In **Mali**, cowpea haulms are also transported to the household. In addition, 53 percent of the farmers in three villages collected bush straw. In **Burkina Faso**, a similar situation exists, although only 32 percent of oxen-owning farmers were reported to be collecting bush straw; 23 percent of these farmers transported sorghum and millet stalks to the household. However, the crop residue situation is acute since the principal cash crop, cotton, provides no edible residues. In addition to crop residues from the fields and straw from the bush around the villages studied in **Niger**, there are substantial fodder markets in the villages and a quarter of the farmers in the survey purchased cowpea or groundnut haulms, while some bought bush straw.

Draft Animals

The use of draft animals is common in the villages studied in Senegal, Mali and Burkina Faso, but rarer in the more arid villages in Niger. The main increase in use occurred under the impact of groundnut production schemes in Senegal and Mali during the 1950s and 1960s, and slightly later in Burkina Faso under the impact of the cotton growing schemes with the support of SOFITEX. Evidence suggests that the principal effect of introducing animal traction is an extension of the area cultivated, with a minimal impact on crop yields per unit area.[28]

In **Senegal**, the principal draft animal is the horse and although SODEVA promoted oxen during the 1970s, few remain in the villages. In the six villages studied there were 1,271 horses but only 284 oxen, 190 of which were in one village. In a separate random sample of eight villages an average of 2.4 horses per household was found. There is an overall shortage of horses in relation to the area cultivated and poorer farmers are obliged to borrow or hire, with adverse consequences on the timeliness of their field operations. The horse is preferred for social, technical, and economic reasons. It can work the light sandy soils in the north faster than oxen. It is also more appropriate as a transport animal being capable of working longer and travelling faster.

The returns to horse traction are higher than those to ox traction **(Table 6)**. The relatively infrequent use of donkeys which are cheaper than horses and consume less feed, but which can perform many of the tasks just as well, can only be explained by social and religious factors. The 1984 drought not only caused high mortality among draft animals, but also drove many poorer farmers to sell their animals and equipment. The principal tasks performed with the aid of draft animals are planting, inter-row cultivation, weeding, harvesting of groundnuts and transport (both of manure and of the harvest).

Table 6. Estimates of Returns Using Draft Animals

Net returns (000 CFA) *Country* *Crop* *Animal*	*Year 1*	*Years 2-4*[a]	*Year 5*[b]	*Net present value at 10%*	*Irr*[c]
Senegal					
Groundnuts (oxen)	-252.5	88.0	391.2	233.5	38%
Groundnuts (horses)	-173.6	76.9	109.2	283.0	43%
Millet (oxen)	-258.5	82.0	335.2	174.4	31%
Millet (horses)	179.6	70.9	103.2	242.2	38%
Mali					
Millet, cowpeas (oxen)	114.5	131.5	371.5	371.5	121%
Burkina Faso					
Cotton (oxen)	29.6	275.6	515.6	1067.1	infinite
Sorghum (oxen)	120.9	125.1	365.1	439.6	109%
Niger					
Millet, cowpeas (oxen)	193.3	58.2	300.6	150.7	34%

a. Years 2 to 9 for cultivation with horses
b. Year 10 for cultivation with horses
c. Internal rate of return
Source: Study reports

In **Mali** oxen are used for ploughing and donkeys for transport. Ownership of oxes varies widely between villages. All of the farmers in a village benefitting from an IFAD-assisted project had oxen, and in another richer village with larger cattle herds and more land, 96 percent of the households owned oxen. In the other three villages only twelve families out of a sample of thirty-seven owned oxen, and hiring and borrowing was common. Donkey ownership was much more widespread. As in Senegal, there are considerable shortages of equipment, and apart from the IFAD-assisted village many farmers have not purchased new equipment since the 1970s.

Both oxen and donkeys are widely used in **Burkina Faso** and the relatively high returns from cotton production have encouraged investment in draft animals and equipment. There were also twenty-nine farmers with tractors in the five villages. However, not all the farmers possess oxen and the high purchase price of oxen, feed scarcity, and high mortality levels have encouraged some farmers to replace them with donkeys.

In three of the villages studied in **Niger** there were only forty-five pairs of oxen and in the other three villages there were no oxen. Ownership of donkeys was more widespread and in one village there were thirty donkeys but no oxen. The ILCA studies in the villages of Fabidji and Goberi, adjacent to the village of Birniel Alfari, indicated a very high utilization of donkeys as compared with oxen, mostly for the transport of manure.

Table 6 presents some derived data from this study pertaining to the costs of animal traction in the four countries, to illustrate the profitability and viability of using draft animals in the various crop cultivation processes. This analysis of returns incorpo rates estimates of (a) the purchase and sales prices of the animals (where horses have a disadvantage in the sense that their "end value" after a working life of ten years is zero, whereas oxen are sold to slaughter for meat production); (b) the costs of equipment (including ploughs, planters and weeders as well as carts purchased on credit); (c) a mortality allowance; (d) veterinary and health costs; (e) feed and herding costs (which are particularly difficult to estimate given the wide range of feedstuffs including natural pasture); and (f) the opportunity costs of labor.

The main benefits from using draft animals and equipment are obtained from the total value (gross revenue) of crop output, less the direct variable costs (of seed, fertilizer and other inputs), plus the value of the manure produced.[29] Evidence suggests that manure output assessed at 300 kg of dry matter per TLU is worth about 6600 CFA per annum. On this basis, the net returns from using draft animals over five years (oxen) and ten years (horses) in connection with crop cultivation in the villages studied were calculated. Although there is a high degree of uncertainty and variability associated with the data in these examples, the analysis shows some orders of magnitude which suggest that the introduction of animal traction makes a significant contribution to average revenues in some locations.

Given the major assumptions on feed quantities and costs and assuming that draft animals are able on an annual basis to work a total of five hectares in Senegal, Mali and Burkina Faso but only four hectares in Niger, this analysis shows that the use of draft oxen for cotton and sorghum production in Burkina Faso and for millet and cowpea production in Mali is profitable. This assumes that the farmer purchases his oxen and equipment from his own resources (and in the absence of rural financial institutions there is no opportunity cost of capital). It is decidedly less profitable to use draft animals in Senegal and in Niger. The use of a horse is more profitable than a pair of oxen in Senegal for both groundnuts and millet, this being consistent with and at least partly causative of the farmers' preference for horses. Where the draft animals and equipment are financed from medium term credit on typical terms then the enterprise is only viable in Burkina Faso and Mali. Only marginal returns are obtained in Senegal using horses, and losses were found in Senegal and Niger using oxen.

Principal Issues in Integration

Expansion or Intensification

One of the main hypotheses underlying this study was that the use of draft animals has led to an expansion of cultivation as opposed to intensification. The evidence from the areas studied strongly indicates that animal traction has contributed to an increase in cultivated areas. This has largely occurred as a result of the introduction of cash crops, profits from which have financed the purchase of draft animals and equipment. This process of expansion occurred when land was abundant in relation to labor, and has taken place in two phases. Initially, virgin uncultivated land was ploughed, and then when the supply was exhausted, land lying fallow was put to the plough. The extension of cultivation has thus been at least partly responsible for the reduction in the use of fallow periods through an increase in cropping intensity.

However, it was not possible to deduce the extent to which the expansion of the area cultivated has also been due to population increases. Nor has it been possible to quantify the extension of cultivation in the villages studied. However, this can be seen in an historical context, since in most of the villages studied there is now a serious land shortage and all available cultivable land is in use. The absence of animal traction in Niger is due to the fact that it is not feasible in the more arid conditions which characterize the area studied. However fallow periods have been greatly reduced and many farmers have no fallow land left.

The question that subsequently arises is what additional income contribution can draft animals provide now that the benefits of higher production and greater farm incomes have been derived from an extension of the cultivated areas. Some partial solutions may be considered. There is scope for the adoption of more equipment to be used with draft animals. Where profitable, as for example on the cotton farms in Burkina Faso, farmers can increase their level of mechanization, thereby reducing unit labor costs, and freeing family labor (if family labor is used) for other income-generating activities. Increased yields through better land preparation may be technically feasible particularly on the heavier soils, but there has been little evidence of this from other parts of the world, but it is unlikely that such improvements in tillage could be achieved with existing draft animals and equipment.

In practice there is some evidence that yield levels are declining on farms in the areas studied due to losing the benefits of timely farming operations being lost. This is related to the shortage of draft animals following the drought and the unfavorable price environment for farmers. On the other hand, there is scope for designing more appropriate equipment, and in particular lighter tools for use by donkeys which appear to be more cost effective than oxen or horses, although they can only be used for cultivation on the sandy soils.

As farm incomes from crop production are declining many farmers seek to supplement them by using draft animals for off-farm transport. The growth in demand for donkeys is largely due to their potential for general transport. Many farmers also indicated that a cart is the most important item of equipment and always the first to be purchased. No data were obtained on the distribution of draft animals and carts between farm activities and non-farm activities. However, the observations during the study suggested that many farmers who own draft animals and carts hire them out in the dry season.

Competition for Land

The process of integration is fuelled by pressure on land resources. There are three scenarios of competition for land in the villages:

- Between end uses: crops versus livestock (grazing)
- Between farmers for crop land: Farmer A (resident) versus Farmer B (immigrant)
- Between livestock owners for village pasture land: Herd A (local mixed crop farmer) versus Herd B (transhumant pastoralist).

The system of land ownership is of paramount importance in the development of integrated farming systems. First, under existing traditional tenure systems in the Sahel, permanent usufruct rights are available only to those settled farmers who cultivate land. Land rights thus concern land cultivated either at present or in the past. Usufruct rights also apply to fallow land. Second, in crop farming areas with high population densities the boundaries of village land are contiguous with those of the neighboring villages, and there is no land which does not belong to a village. Residual uncultivated land for which there are no usufruct rights is communal grazing land, yet it remains village land, and if required for village activities access to it can be controlled.

Expansion of cultivated land has always been at the expense of the best grazing land, and thus communal grazing areas have not only become smaller but also less productive per unit area. In addition, access to village communal grazing areas by transhumant herders was allowed in the past because under the previous system of interaction between herders and crop farmers this was in the best interests of both groups. With the growth in the numbers of village livestock, this communal grazing area is now required for village stock. Since it forms part of the village land, livestock in the village have prior rights of access.

Two systems of village land tenure are of particular importance in understanding the competition for land. The first is the permanent usufruct granted to an individual for land cultivated, and the second is the village control over the residual uncultivated areas within the village boundaries. In the competition between crops and livestock, crops will always "win." In the competition for pasture, between crop farmers stock and pastoralist stock, the former always "wins." In the latter competitive scenario, concerning access to crop land between resident and immigrant, the resident will always come first since the immigrant can only have access to land when there is enough to meet the requirements of both, and the former has the muscle to enforce this dominance.

In many of the villages studied the shortage of crop land is a relatively recent phenomenon. Not only is it becoming scarcer, but given the declining fallow periods, it is also becoming less fertile. Land has become the most valuable resource in most villages and access to land for cultivation has become a key element in household survival strategies. This has led to increased borrowing by households which do not have permanent access to sufficient land, and frequently such borrowed land is that which would otherwise lie fallow. At present most borrowing takes place within the extended family and repayment is in kind. Only one example of a farmer renting land for cash was encountered in the study, where the two parties belonged to different ethnic groups. But as land becomes scarcer a rental market for land may develop.

In all the villages, an increasing number of often violent conflicts over access to land were noted. This is to some extent inevitable as competition for land increases and since the traditional system of obtaining usufruct is by verbal agreement with the *Chef de Terre*, which can be misinterpreted. Problems frequently arise at the boundaries between fields. Also owners of land which has been lent out often have difficulty recovering their land from the borrower who may claim "squatters rights."

Thus the scarcity of land has three facets, (a) declining soil fertility as fallow periods are reduced; (b) increasing conflict as competition for land intensifies and as land rights are not clearly defined; and (c) rising land values leading to greater household emphasis on securing and maintaining access to land, with more and more households dependent on borrowing land. The issue of land tenure is now widely recognized to be a major problem which must be tackled in the development of sustainable integrated farming in the Sahel through the introduction of land use management schemes and appropriate legislation.[30]

The Future of Transhumant Pastoralism

Competition for the use of village pastures is of vital importance because it has major implications for the future of transhumant pastoral livestock systems. Given the scarcity of pasture in many parts of the Sahel, many pastoralists are obliged to abandon their traditional dry season grazing areas and move elsewhere. At present there are still some villages with available pasture (although not in the area studied), and further south in higher rainfall zones both pasture production and crop residue output is greater. Although many transhumant herds are moving further south in the dry season, this exposes them to the risk of trypanosomiasis.

The decline in transhumant pastoralism is widespread in the Sahel. The proportion of total stock owned by transhumant pastoralists has declined sharply and most animals are now owned by the original arable farmers. The combined effects of drought, poor terms of trade between livestock and crops, and declining pasture availability have all resulted in major changes in livestock ownership and production systems.[31]

In the long term, transhumant production systems may be restricted to the low rainfall pastoral areas where crop farming is marginal. The alternative is for transhumant pastoralists to settle and cultivate the land, thereby producing crop residues for their livestock. By settling and cultivating they may be able to obtain permanent usufruct rights to the land they cultivate, and also establish their presence as permanent members of a community with rights to exploit the residual village grazing areas. Evidence from the villages studied suggests that they are increasingly settling and cultivating. Furthermore, the proportion of their stock practicing transhumance beyond village boundaries is declining, as they increasingly seek feed from crop residues and village pastures.

Another basic hypothesis of the study was that the integration of livestock and crop production systems will increase cereals production and income for the farmers, at the same time promoting the rehabilitation of pastoral range lands. There is no doubt that the first part of this hypothesis is valid. Through animal traction and through the use of manure, livestock have contributed enormously to both increased cereals production and farm incomes. Nevertheless, if the increased production has been obtained through an extension of cultivation which has shortened fallow periods, then the long-term benefits may be compromised. Evidence to support the latter part of the hypothesis on pastoral rehabilitation is lacking. The pastoral areas of crop farming villages are communally owned and are overexploited. Previously such overstocking was by transhumant herds. Now it is by village herds.

The integration process involves the livestock owned by predominantly arable farmers and not the livestock of transhumant pastoralists (unless they settle and become crop farmers), and the latter progressively lose access to village pastures as the village stock take precedence. As cropping zone pastures are increasingly denied to transhumant pastoralists they will become more dependent on the sparse pastures in the northern rangelands. Without measures to protect and control this pasture resource it will be overexploited by pastoralists obliged to keep their stock in the northern areas throughout the year. Thus the adoption of integration practices in the cropping zone is likely to have a negative impact on the pastoral rangelands. Stock numbers will be substantially reduced as these pasture resources cannot by themselves support the numbers which presently benefit from a transhumant system using both crop zone pastures and pastoral rangelands. The maintenance of optimum production conditions for transhumant livestock, as in the case of crop cultivation systems, will require defined rights to pasture and water for all groups of livestock owners in the different agro-ecological zones. But, as legislative initiatives have shown, this is not an easy task.[32]

Fertilization of Agricultural Land

Improving the fertility of the fragile soils of the Sahel is the most important issue in the integration of livestock in crop cultivation systems. Soil fertility is a synthesis of a number of factors including soil depth, texture, organic matter content and nutrient replenishment. The experience of some cotton farmers in Mali who have applied only chemical fertilizers for many years without adding organic matter and have now been obliged to abandon their fields, indicates the need to maintain both macro-nutrients in inorganic fertilizer, as well as organic matter which also contains micro-nutrients (and fibre which improves soil texture).

However, the solution to the problem of soil impoverishment need not involve livestock. The incorporation of sown legume fallows may serve just as well as manure, although the increasing pressure on grazing land may make this a less than practicable option. Using harvesting techniques which keep the roots in the soil and minimum sow-tillage techniques which do not expose soil organic matter to as much oxidation are preferable options. Agro-forestry, using deep rooted trees as nutrient pumps is another viable option under certain circumstances. The IRCT in Burkina Faso has estimated a loss of 600 kg of organic matter per hectare per annum from the top 20 cm of soil alone. Since the organic matter content in these cultivated soils is already low, priority must be given to reversing this trend.

Farmers in the areas studied are increasingly applying manure from their night paddocks and using household residues. But those who obtained supplies from large transhumant herds in exchange for crop products in the past, now find that the manure from their own livestock is insufficient. That farmers understand the value of manure is beyond doubt, and they are using more and more of their labor to transport and spread manure on fields. However, farmers probably effectively capture and use less than 50 percent of the manure produced by their animals. Substantial improvements can be achieved, first, by capturing all the manure produced. This requires year-round night paddocking and as much stable feeding as possible. Alternatively, farmers can employ the "moving barn" technique during the day on fields close to the village, tethering and "zero-grazing" their livestock. In this way urine and manure are deposited on the soil with the animals being moved to fresh soil on a regular basis to ensure an even spread over a given field. Farmers can also compost manure with straw from the bush or from the inedible parts of sorghum and millet stover, a practice which could increase manure use from an estimated 500-600 kg per annum per TLU to between four and five tons.

Sustainable Production Systems

Sustainable soil fertility is at the core of the analysis of viable production systems. The conclusion from the analysis of production systems in the villages is that the present system is not sustainable. There is a continuous loss both of minerals and organic matter as a result of the reduced, and in some areas, total abandonment of fallow periods. But farmers are generally aware of the declining soil fertility and are trying to maximize manure use both from their own herds as well as from transhumant herds where they still exist. Inorganic fertilizer application which addresses only macro-nutrient deficiencies (and often insufficiently), is only viable on the cotton crop given the present low farmgate price levels of the crops. As noted above, it appears that the quantities of manure applied by farmers are not sufficient to maintain soil organic matter levels which, without adequate fallow periods, are steadily declining.

To maintain organic matter at acceptable levels for continuous crop cultivation would require an estimated minimum of two tons of manure per hectare per annum. Given an approximate manure supply of 300 kg per TLU under present production systems, seven mature cattle are required to produce this quantity. Edible dry matter production of millet or sorghum stover is estimated at 700-900 kg per hectare in the 500-700 mm rainfall zone. With a total daily dry matter requirement of 2.5 percent of body weight (250 kg) for six months, and 2 percent for the six months dry season, total dry matter required for seven cattle would be fourteen tons per annum. Stover from one hectare of millet or sorghum would provide just 6 percent of this requirement and the rest must be provided by natural pastures. Assuming an edible dry matter output of 600 kg per hectare from the pastures (and no bush fires) then twenty-three hectares would be required to feed sufficient cattle to provide manure to maintain fertility on one hectare of cultivated land. In much of the Sahelian region such pasture areas are not available, and the ratio of twenty-three hectares needed to keep one hectare adequately manured is clearly quite impossible, especially bearing in mind the labor and transport requirements.

The demand for cropping land is further increased by declining yields which force farmers to seek additional land in compensation. The inescapable conclusion is that the land and soil resources cannot support the present human and animal populations without a quantum leap in the amount of inorganic fertilizer used, or soil fertility improvement in some other way. This conclusion is borne out in many of the villages studied where acute land shortages are leading to the gradual abandonment of farming by many of the poorer villagers.[33]

Use of Crop Residues

In the Sahel the stover from millet and sorghum is presently being used for at least four different purposes: as feed for livestock, for incorporation in the soil in order to restore fertility, as domestic fuel for cooking, and for fencing and other building activities. In the areas studied, most stover was used for animal feed, although much of the stover left on the fields was wastefully browsed or grazed. A trend towards the transport of stover to the household was noted. All groundnut and cowpea residues were transported and fed to stock at the household reflecting their higher value. Where stover was left on the field the inedible parts were invariably burnt before land preparation for the following crop, thus losing not only some of their nutrients but also all of their organic matter. There was no evidence of stover being used for domestic fuel in the villages, but millet stalks were used for fencing.

Farmers are aware of the rising value of stover as indicated by the increasing practice of transporting and storing it, but considerable increases in the quantity consumed can be obtained through improved storage, feeding practices (stalls) and through treatment with urea and water. The introduction of techniques to chop stover can also result in improved consumption and digestibility. At present only about 30 percent of the stover is edible.

Constraints Limiting Livestock Production

The case for integrating livestock into crop production systems rests on the premise that the by-products of the two systems are both utilized on the same farm thus contributing to overall higher output. The objective is to intensify production in order to secure higher levels of output per animal and per hectare. The trend towards permanent stabling of stock as observed in the villages is a move towards intensification. By feeding a balanced diet of farm-produced fodder, both milk and meat output per animal can be increased in relation to the present semi-extensive system. However a smaller number of livestock could perhaps produce an output equivalent to that of the present system. But a number of constraints limit more intensive livestock production, three of which are as follows:

First, intensification requires high labor inputs which will reduce incentives until output prices rise in relation to the opportunity cost of family labor.

Second, the lack of alternative investment opportunities encourages farmers to overstock, thereby leading to continuous and accelerated degradation of their pastures. Most village based livestock are not "productive" , being primarily acquired or maintained for the purpose of raising farm production, or farm incomes. Rather they serve as a reserve of capital which can be called on in times of drought, or for social or prestige purposes. There are few alternative investment opportunities for settled farmers to use their surplus revenues, and investment in livestock has always been a traditional method of keeping capital. One consequence of this is that many farmers keep many more livestock than can be efficiently integrated into the farm production systems. Excess stock which cannot be fed on crop residues must be maintained on village pastures which without grazing control are frequently overexploited. The establishment of alternative investment opportunities is urgently required, and the creation of village level financial institutions to provide both security and an attractive return should be vigorously pursued.

Third, most farmers are still very ignorant about feeding and stock management. The feed and water requirements for different types of stock are not well known, and investment in teaching basic animal husbandry to farmers would be valuable. Where livestock can be maintained on farm-produced fodder without overexploiting natural pastures then intensification, if economically viable, should be promoted since it contributes to the production of more meat and milk.

Integration Practices to Increase Farm Incomes

There are four ways to promote further integration by which farm incomes can be increased.

a. Measures which enable farmers to use manure more efficiently by capturing a higher proportion of total manure output and then composting it with unpalatable crop stover. These activities involve additional labor inputs. Transporting and spreading manure are dry season activities, but most family labor is usually engaged in some non-agricultural activity.

b. Direct encouragement of farmers to produce more fodder and to store and use the fodder already produced more efficiently. The transport and correct storage of crop residues, stover from millet and sorghum, and groundnut and cowpea haulms, should be promoted. More attention should be given to developing varieties of groundnuts and cowpeas with good stalk and hay production. Many farmers prefer such varieties of both groundnuts (in Senegal), and of cowpeas (in Mali and Niger). Where fodder is very scarce, as for example in Burkina Faso and in parts of Mali, the introduction of specialized fodder crops may be viable.

c. Provision of draft animals and equipment. As mentioned, various opportunities lie in developing more appropriate equipment, and in assisting farmers to utilize their animals and carts in the transport sector, thus diversifying their sources of income.

d. Finally, schemes to develop more efficient fattening programs, especially of small ruminants, would be particularly beneficial.[34]

Polarization of Farm Incomes

Wide variations in levels of income, wealth and household size are found in all the villages studied. Cash incomes from crop production are almost entirely restricted to farmers growing groundnuts in Senegal and cotton in Burkina Faso. As noted above, many households do not produce sufficient cereals to meet their domestic requirements.

Incomes from livestock fluctuate considerably on account of drought, while the stagnant prices due to competition on export markets in the West African coastal countries from cheap beef (imported from the EC and Latin America) have also adversely affected earnings from livestock production. Furthermore, the declining productivity of natural pastures and the scarcity of fodder have contributed to high mortality rates.

Therefore, many farmers seek to diversify their incomes to protect their assets against loss from drought or external economic factors. Off-farm income has become increasingly important, and all the farmers in the villages studied in Senegal, Mali and Niger have some sources of off-farm income.[35] Only the cotton farmers in Burkina Faso obtain most of their income from crop production alone. The contribution of crop production to household incomes in Mali is extremely low, and in the poorer villages the main sources of cash income include the (illegal) cutting of firewood, migrants remittances and the raising of small ruminants.

The evidence suggests that a process of polarization of household incomes is occurring with richer farmers increasing their assets, largely at the expense of the poorer farmers who are becoming even poorer; some are eventually forced to abandon farming. The richer farmers invest in other income-generating assets, thereby diversifying income potential, and are thus better armed to withstand the impact of drought or other exogenous shocks. Poorer farmers, unable to produce sufficient cereals to meet their domestic requirements, are obliged to sell off assets, such as small ruminants (when the price is low) in order to buy cereals.

The introduction of animal traction has contributed substantially to the process of income polarization. Wealthy farmers with draft animals have been able to increase farm incomes through increasing the area cultivated, enabling them to diversify their assets, for example by investing in different types of livestock, by obtaining additional labor through marriage, and by investing in non-farm activities such as transport facilities. They have also increased their income by establishing markets for draft animals and equipment, further reinforcing income disparities.

5. *Development - With or Without Intervention*

Non-Intervention Scenarios

Possible forms of intervention designed to promote and strengthen the integration of crop and livestock production in the Sahel are addressed in the second section of this chapter. This first section briefly indicates the possible evolution of the farming systems in the region if there is no outside intervention. Their dynamic nature is an important concept as there are continuously changing responses to different supply and demand patterns in factor and output markets, as well as changing responses to climatic fluctuations. In general, the dominant relationship will be the declining area (and quality) of land in relation to a steadily increasing population, leading to an intensification of land use.

Non-intervention scenarios largely reflect trends which are already clearly visible in the study areas.[36] The principal characteristics of the processes observed are as follows:

- The availability and productivity of existing natural pastures will continue to decline unless there is a marked upward shift in average rainfall levels, or a system of rational exploitation can be established to avoid overstocking. The former is unpredictable, and the latter requires such radical changes in traditional land use systems, land rights and other social processes that it is unlikely to occur within the next few years.

- Transhumant livestock herding will be progressively excluded from crop cultivation areas because the settled village herds have a prior claim to village pastures. Livestock farmers will adopt strategies to discourage transhumant herds, by restricting access to water, by pre-emptive grass cutting, and so on. This has extremely serious consequences for the future of pastoral livestock systems. In the long term they can exist only in the Sahelian and Sahelo-Saharan zones where the average annual rainfall is less than about 350 mm.

- The processes of integration and intensification of crop and livestock production systems will continue because declining feed resources and soil fertility will raise the economic value of both farm-produced fodder and manure. This increase in value, which may or may not be reflected in market prices (it is already for fodder), will ensure that farmers will use residues and manure more efficiently. Specifically, the trend towards increased collection and storing of crop residues at the household will continue, since farmers will aim for their maximum utilization. Similarly, in order to collect as much manure as possible for fertilizing the fields, the use of night paddocks for manure collection will increase. Total livestock numbers in the villages will increase as greater use of crop residues permits higher stocking rates.

- The above pressures will encourage the trend towards maintaining more livestock at the household. They will be further reinforced by the rising cost of labor for herding, since such domestically maintained animals will not require herding except for watering at the village well. This trend towards intensification is inevitable given the declining pasture resources.
- The practice of cutting bush grasses and transporting them to the household (or to market for sale) will continue, as many livestock owners do not have sufficient crop residues to carry their stock through the dry season. As the practice of cutting this grass becomes more widespread, there will also be competition for this resource. Since it is found on common land, there will be a tendency to cut progressively earlier which has the advantage that the nutritional value of the straw is better retained. Ideally, it should be cut green and stored as hay, but this is not likely since labor at this period is not available and it is difficult to dry the hay.
- Fallow periods throughout the region will continue to decline and will ultimately disappear.
- If producer prices for cash crops remain low, then incomes will also remain low. The combination of lower unit production costs and stable farmgate prices for cotton in Burkina Faso may maintain cotton incomes at present levels, but the outlook for groundnut producers is not encouraging.[37]
- Producer prices for cereals are expected to fluctuate, often quite dramatically, as relatively small changes in output cause big swings in price. Unless there are improvements in the primary marketing of cereals, seasonal and spatial price variations will be large. Small producers will suffer most from such variations. The main reason for big price fluctuations is the climate. Further major droughts can and should be expected.
- The inefficiencies in the present marketing system for cereals are likely to persist with unfavorable consequences especially for small farmers. As farm incomes remain depressed, the need to diversify will increase and more families will seek additional off-farm income. The economic polarization between rich farmers who are owners of assets (land, labor, draft animals, transport equipment, and so forth), and poor families without assets is likely to increase. The number of families obliged to abandon farming will also increase.

This scenario presents many challenges in terms of competition between different activities and groups of people and in terms of the use of resources in the Sahel. It also illustrates the complexity of the vicious circle of constraints which affect the comparative advantages within the agricultural sector in these countries. The task is to devise, and then facilitate implementation of, appropriate and financially viable measures which will ensure both efficient resource use and improvements in farm incomes. These issues, and proposals which could contribute to developing agricultural production techniques, are outlined in the following section.

Intervention Approaches

Integration and the Management of Resources

The fundamental problem of resource management in the Sahel has gradually assumed increased importance, in connection with the development of crop and livestock production systems, and in connection with efforts to reverse the trend towards greater environmental degradation. Major intervention is required to arrest the degradation of arable land, natural pastures, and forests in many areas. These are complex tasks because they involve both wholehearted village participation and government involvement.[38]

The thorny issue of use and control of land is the key. Although, collectively, a village community may adopt a new resource management plan designed to improve pasture and wood production through rotational grazing, the introduction of new species and so on, the plan will fail unless the villagers can protect their land from exploitation by transhumant herders, illegal wood cutters and others. The ability to protect land which is communally owned is lacking and this is a major obstacle to improved resource use. Unless governments and the rural communities which they represent are committed to protecting village land against abuse, it will be hard to ensure that rehabilitation measures succeed. Furthermore, the statutory definition of user rights and the adoption of adequate legislation to ensure equitable land tenure systems are vital components of resource management schemes.

In villages where land for cultivation and grazing is becoming scarce, particular emphasis should be attached to creating an awareness of the consequences of overexploitation. Villagers generally have their own perceptions of the scale and causes of deterioration in natural resources, declining crop yields, depletion of forest cover, and degradation of pasture. Technically, there are a number of options available to increase production from pastures and forest areas such as rotational grazing, elimination of (or controlled) burning, introduction of new species, and so forth. Other soil and water conservation techniques and schemes to improve environmental protection have been introduced in numerous villages throughout the Sahel with varying degrees of success.[39] There is considerable scope for socio-technical assessment of existing methods and devising new approaches to increase production. Such schemes may be costly to implement in relation to the contribution which can be made by the communities concerned, but the long-term environmental and economic benefits as well as potential knock-on effects in neighboring areas may justify a major contribution by donor agencies.

Farm Specific Interventions

A number of specific measures to increase farm productivity through crop and livestock integration can be envisaged. The studies carried out in the selected villages revealed various initiatives which have been launched on the basis of technical and financial support through a wide range of different external agencies including both local and foreign ngos as well as official development institutions.[40] Some of the appropriate technologies and problems of implementation are outlined below.

FERTILIZATION OF FIELDS. Top priority should be given to reversing the present declining soil fertility due to reduced fallow periods, since this has a direct impact through crop yields on food supplies and on farm incomes. It is also at the core of the problem of achieving a sustainable production system.[41] Most farmers are aware of declining fertility and already appreciate the economic value of manure. Measures to increase the quantity applied by collecting the total output of animals, and composting manure with crop residues, straw or other green material which are unpalatable to livestock, should be encouraged. Further on-farm pilot schemes should be initiated, building on the experience from the "parcs d'hivernage" (rainy season) in Burkina Faso. This experience in Burkina Faso indicates that two-ton dry matter of mixed manure sorghum stover compost containing 30 percent organic matter are required to maintain the organic matter level on one hectare of land cultivated every year. Composting takes place by cattle trampling and crushing the stover bedding to which their manure is added. The compost is left during the rainy season to mature and is applied in the following crop year. Three cattle are required to produce about 500 kg dry matter of manure during the 150 day dry season after the sorghum harvest. Where the composting takes place near the household, considerable time and labor are involved in transport of residues to the household and compost to the field. Water should be added to accelerate decomposition, increasing the labor requirements. The vigorous promotion of more efficient manure use and composting techniques is important.

Other techniques for raising the organic matter and nutrient content of fields include the cultivation of edible legume crops either in association with millet as in Niger and Mali, or in pure stands as land otherwise left fallow. But where fallow periods have largely disappeared the use of pure legume stands could only be achieved by depriving farmers of land for immediate staple cereal production. This would further accelerate the exodus from the land. Should such a strategy be adopted, it may be necessary to compensate for land taken out of food production and put under fallow, by providing cereals or cash to buy them. In reality this would be very difficult to implement socially and could easily be abused.[42]

In the relatively few locations where the organic matter content of the soil is high enough, appropriate use of inorganic fertilizer could be justified if the expected yield response provides incremental revenue to more than offset the cost of its purchase. However, the risk of crop failure due to drought is high and many farmers prefer not to use fertilizers until substantial rains have commenced during the growing season when the risk of crop failure is less. Fertilizer can then be applied only as a top dressing, instead of as a base dressing before planting. The latter is essential for the relatively insoluble phosphatic fertilizer which needs to have direct contact with the plant roots for the benefits to be derived.

Increasing animal feed supplies. In order to increase livestock productivity, a wide range of measures could be introduced which contribute to increasing the supply of animal feed.

- The adoption of cowpea varieties which, in addition to high grain yields, also give good haulm yields should be encouraged. Evidence from the study villages suggests that farmers already prefer such varieties. In all countries where they are marketed, leguminous haulm prices appear to be rising more rapidly than grain prices.
- The collection and storage of all farm-produced fodder can be improved by transporting it to the household and storing it under cover from the sun. Any residual millet and sorghum stover could be incorporated in a manure compost. At present such non-edible residues are left on fields where they may be eaten by termites, and they are usually burnt before ploughing the following season with consequent loss both of nitrogen and of organic matter.
- The edible proportion of sorghum and millet stover can be increased from about 30 percent to about 60 percent by chopping. Manual chopping equipment should be tested and promoted. Stall feeding rather than ground spreading also reduces the trampling and spoilage of fodder.
- The practice of cutting grass from natural pastures, now widespread in all

four countries, should be encouraged and the grass should be properly stored. Correct storage has been successfully introduced in one of the villages studied in Niger. The increased cutting of grass in the pasture and lightly forested areas will reduce the risk of destructive bush fires and will have significant environmental benefits. Such practices require additional labor, but as fodder prices rise they will become more financially attractive. However, the collection of straw for settled herds will reduce its availability for transhumant herds, unless the pastoralists can negotiate special access.

- There is very encouraging evidence from Mali and Burkina Faso that some farmers, and in particular the Fulani, are willing to adopt the production of specific fodder crops such as *Dolichos lablab* or *Siratro*, as partial solutions to the problem of feed scarcity. At present, the principal constraints are the high opportunity costs of land and labor, the high cost of imported seed, lack of information about cultivation techniques and the high cost of protecting the fodder areas during the first few years while live hedges around them are established. On the FAO/CILSS fodder crop project in Mali, yields of *Dolichos lablab* varied between 928 kg/ha of dry matter and 1,654 kg/ha depending on whether manure, phosphate or a composite NPK fertilizer is added. The viability of fodder crop production depends largely on fodder prices. As indicated above, these have been rising rapidly and fodder crop production will become increasingly profitable. An aspect of this is that fodder prices are subject to wide seasonal variation, increasing by as much as five times between the harvest and the onset of the following rains. Not only do such crops provide valuable fodder but as legumes they contribute to maintaining soil fertility. Further fodder crop production is to be encouraged. High yielding fodder crops could become major cash crops in milk-producing areas near urban centers.

- Increasing the energy intake of specific animals, especially lactating cows, draft animals, calves at risk, and, animals being fattened for slaughter could be achieved by greater use of agro-industrial by-products such as molasses in a form which is easily transportable and palatable. The introduction of fabricated blocks (*melure*), containing molasses, urea, rice husks and salt in Mali is an excellent development and similar schemes should be initiated where possible, to take advantage of the high energy content of molasses (a product which appears to be available in many areas). A further additive is urea which when mixed with straw or crop residues (not only by itself) can increase nitrogen intake and can also increase energy intake through increasing the digestibility of straw. Urea enrichment has been successfully introduced in Mali in certain selected villages in the West Sahel Livestock Development Project. Twelve kg of urea per cow fed in a 4 percent mixture over sixty days costing less than US$6 produced average weight gains of 11 kg in an ILCA trial. Care is required in the proportions used and in ensuring good quality straw.

- There is considerable ignorance among farmers about feeding requirements. Many farmers still aim for the minimum-cost feed strategy and then complain when their animals die. A major educational program should be undertaken by the technical agents of a local development organization or by agents of government livestock services, who are still predominantly veterinarians rather than general husbandry staff.

FATTENING OF STOCK. Assuming that there is a sufficient price differential of saleable stock between the start and the end of the dry season in the principal slaughter markets, fattening of both sheep and oxen is profitable. Sheep fattening is more profitable, because less feed is required to produce the same quantity of meat than for cattle. Mortality risks and capital costs are also lower. Since it is a dry season activity, undertaken mostly by women and children whose opportunity cost is relatively low then, it represents an efficient use of resources. Women are often owners of small ruminants which are a means of raising their incomes. However many farmers fail to deworm their stock and thus do not get the full benefits of the feed.

Fattening schemes for small ruminants can increase the incomes of poorer farmers, and thereby counteract the present trend towards increased social stratification. Fattening of oxen and bulls is more risky and is not appropriate for small farmers. Furthermore, small ruminants can be transported by pick-up in substantial numbers whereas the transport of cattle is mostly on foot, with risk of weight losses and disease.

DRAFT ANIMALS AND EQUIPMENT. The use of draft animals, especially horses and donkeys, for transport in conjunction with a cart appears to be highly profitable. The donkey is the most efficient transport animal, with purchase costs and feed requirements which are substantially less than those of horses and oxen. Rental markets for donkeys and carts for transport are widespread and good profits can be made from this investment. Yet there is a danger that in some villages the numbers of donkeys (or horses) and carts may exceed the demand for their use.

In practice animals are used both for cultivation and for transport, and the benefits from the latter may offset any losses from cultivation. Any proposed investment should be carefully analyzed to assess the overall demand for the use of the animals and equipment. However, where draft animals and equipment are hired out they may contribute to income disparities within the community.

OTHER ON-FARM INTERVENTIONS. Apart from measures directly related to crop and livestock integration, there are many other possible approaches to increasing production. Encouraging farmers to produce their own woodlots or live hedges, or to undertake soil and water conservation measures similar to those which have been successfully introduced in a number of different locations throughout the Sahel are examples of such practical measures which can have major crop yield and income benefits. Introducing better seeds and equipment are further examples. Evidence suggests that appropriate and successful pilot schemes which focus on individual farmers may lead to rapid multiplication effects whenever the members of a community are able to gain immediate material benefits.

Complementary Rural Development Activities

There is also a wide range of activities which can be initiated by local development organizations, from the "bottom up". But some of the most important services, including credit and savings facilities, input delivery systems, marketing arrangements, extension services (including veterinary), adult literacy programs, health services, training schemes and water supply programs are presently subject to major reforms in the context of economic adjustment programs.[43]

In the following discussion, priority is given to credit and savings facilities, because the existing services are extremely weak or non-existent in the Sahel. This lack has contributed substantially to low levels of farm income, and increased the risks entailed through crop and livestock production. The provision of such services is one of the most effective methods of raising farm incomes. The principal costs involved are for manpower and training.

CREDIT AND SAVINGS. With the exception of the credit scheme for cotton farmers in Burkina Faso, large official credit schemes have failed in the countries studied. But many poorer smallholders need credit to buy seeds or fertilizers because of cash flow problems during the year. The provision of credit to such farmers is highly risky. They usually lack collateral and may also lack the resources or knowledge to make efficient use of credit. Hence, credit must be tailor-made to the individual requirements of each farmer, taking account of land, animals, equipment and family labor endowments, and of income diversification and survival strategies. Credit should only be provided where a clearly identifiable source of income exists from which repayment can be made. The manpower requirements for effective use of credit especially by poorer farmers are very substantial, because the credit must be accompanied by technical, managerial and financial advice. Provision of credit for uniform packages is not recommended.

Savings facilities are also urgently required in which farmers can deposit their funds after the harvest, or after the sale of animals. They need to have confidence in the people managing their savings, and the process of depositing and withdrawing must not be too bureaucratic or time-consuming. Ideally, the facility should exist in each village. To be attractive it should provide a return on savings, competitive with the return from investing in livestock, which in the current absence of saving facilities serves as a source of ready capital. Such investment in livestock represents a waste of scarce resources since the animals have low productivity and the conversion of limited fodder supplies into milk and meat is inefficient. And as mentioned above it also contributes to overstocking of natural pastures and resource degradation.

The creation of rural financial institutions able to provide a safe haven for surplus funds could make a major contribution to alleviating the pressure on pasture resources and could provide substantial major environmental benefits. To achieve this asset transfer would require a considerable educational effort to convince farmers of its wisdom, as well as significant investment in training and mobilizing the skilled manpower to operate efficient rural banking services.[44]

INPUT DELIVERY. With the abolition of state-run input delivery systems, the private sector has assumed additional responsibilities. There is little commercial incentive for delivering what are frequently small quantities to remote villages over poor roads. Where undertaken the prices charged are often exorbitant. Where there are no inputs in a village, farmers have to transport them from a distant village or town at high cost. In some of the villages studied important inputs were not available at all. However the benefits of input delivery systems in relation to the costs of providing such services must be carefully assessed.

MARKETING. Primary marketing of most cereals, and groundnuts in Mali, Burkina Faso, and Niger, is in the private sector. In normal years some villages produce a small surplus for sale. But many poor farmers are obliged to sell some of their harvest to repay debts and loans, even though they know that they will be obliged to repurchase grain later in the year when prices may have doubled. Farmgate prices for cereals were low in the late 1980s, given adequate stocks and good harvests. But individual farmers who sell small quantities have little bargaining power, especially when their cash requirements are urgent.

The creation and support of village marketing associations which can accumulate cereals for sale, store them and negotiate bulk sales with traders at a time when prices are higher can lead to substantially higher prices paid to farmers. Furthermore, such marketing organizations can resell grain to farmers later in the year at a lower price than that of the cereal merchants. The benefits from establishing such village "cereal banks" stem from the higher level of farm incomes obtained through intervention in the marketing process.[45] But these organizations also require levels of technical support and management which are usually underestimated. They are also risky. Cereal traders may adopt pricing strategies to ensure that they fail; powerful village interests may combine to influence their operations to the detriment of particular groups of villagers, and they need to have very good market information to ensure that they do not incur losses on their transactions. The costs of their supervision are high and they require literate and numerate villagers to participate in their management. But despite these drawbacks, initiatives of this kind may be important in enabling rural producers to organize and operate in the rural markets.[46]

EXTENSION SERVICES. To increase productivity both in crop production and livestock, farmers require more frequent and better advice on the application of the appropriate cost effective technologies. There are many ways to increase productivity and farmers need advice on which technologies are most likely to be successful and how they should be used; for example, advice on fertilization of fields, more efficient use of manure, introduction of seeds of higher yielding varieties, production and storage of fodder, and advice on feeding and management of stock. The provision of this advice by local development organizations should complement that of existing government extension services which may not have the manpower or resources to undertake it.

Financing Integration

At this point it is necessary to briefly consider the financial implications of the various measures proposed to support the development of integrated farming systems in the Sahel. It has proven difficult to make accurate estimates of the viability of different techniques in terms of returns on investment in the uncertain economic environment faced by crop cultivators and livestock herders in this region. Furthermore, schemes designed to increase animal feed supplies or to improve the use of cultivation equipment may involve additional family labor inputs which even in the dry season may have significant opportunity costs in relation to nonagricultural activities. Interventions to protect the natural resource base and to enhance soil fertility are two obvious examples where individual farmers would be unwilling to sacrifice short-term income gains for long term production benefits.

Substantial investment is required to support the protection of communal pastures and woodlots, but there is also an economic case for providing subsidies to farmers to increase the soil fertility. Present crop production systems without adequate fallow periods involve a continuous loss of nutrients and organic matter from the soil. This loss is not reflected in the farmers costs, yet it has an economic cost. Among the various measures which could be beneficial, but which entail considerable costs (both in initial investment and recurrent repairs, training, and so forth), are:

- The excavation, construction, and correct utilization of compost pits,
- The provision of donkey carts (and possibly donkeys) to facilitate transport of raw materials to compost pits, and of compost to fields,
- The provision of water tanks to be mounted on carts for water transport,

- The provision of grain equivalent to the output of an area taken out of production to lie fallow or sown to green manure legume crops,
- The provision of building materials to construct storage facilities for crop residues and straw from natural pasture,
- The provision of fencing materials to construct night paddocks (*kraals*) on fields or around the villages, thereby promoting more village-based (and household-fed) livestock, and
- The provision of manual feed choppers to increase the proportion of edible sorghum and millet stover available.

To some extent it may be possible to introduce these and numerous other measures on the basis of local savings. Communal village development activities could be financed with contributions both from the village and local development organizations. Many such activities require substantial labor inputs which ought to be provided by the villagers. However the present study indicates that in many villages there are households which have neither the cash nor the labor to contribute and are nearly destitute. Thus, it is essential to consider targeting support programs and financial assistance (for the purchase of inputs, and so forth) in order to develop farming systems and to compensate for the economic loss of soil nutrients and organic matter.[47]

Regional Policy

Finally, it is important to note that improving the productivity of agriculture and the competitiveness of food, cash crop, and animal production in the Sahel necessitates the development of markets on a regional basis in West Africa to maximize the benefits complementary between the different zones. Adjustment policies should incorporate this important dimension, so that it is possible to design investment strategies for the agricultural sector on the basis of regional demand patterns. The development of farming systems in the Sahel has been penalized by disadvantageous terms of trade for many products. Coherent regional agricultural policies, which build on the existing trade network in West Africa, may be a significant complement to more specific measures directed towards intensifying food, cash crop and animal production in the rural communities.

6. Conclusions

Towards Integrated Farming Systems

The shortage of land has become the major production constraint in the region. Competition for land takes three forms, between crop use and pasture use, between crop land for residents and crop land for immigrants, and between pasture for village livestock and pasture for transhumant livestock. Under prevailing land tenure conditions in the Sahel, usufruct rights to land are allocated to cultivators, thus crop land takes priority over pasture, and the best pasture lands are progressively cultivated. Immigrants can only obtain usufruct rights to land where there is sufficient both for residents and immigrants. Borrowing land is frequent but often leads to conflict when the owner wishes to reclaim it. Residual uncultivated village land is available for communal grazing, but village livestock has prior access to it over transhumant livestock because it is still village land. Village boundaries in the areas studied are contiguous and there is no unclaimed land between villages. Given this pattern of use, the intensification of production in conjunction with integrated farming systems represents an important means of enhancing the productivity of the agricultural sector.

However, with the present rate of population growth, pressure on the land is undermining the development of sustainable agricultural production. Soil fertility is continually declining, partly as a result of reduced, and in some areas, totally abandoned fallow periods. Neither minerals nor organic matter are incorporated in the soil during placement and the quantities of manure at present being applied are totally inadequate. Fertilizer use is only viable on the cotton crop, given the present unfavorable farmgate prices of other crops. Even with more efficient manure use it is not possible to maintain organic matter levels unless there are substantial pasture areas from which organic matter can be transferred. With present production systems it is estimated that about twenty-three hectares of natural pasture would be required to produce sufficient manure to maintain organic matter on one hectare for continuous cropping. Such pasture areas are not available in the cropping zone of the Sahel. The introduction of legume fallows although potentially providing a technical solution, would deprive farmers of land for immediate cereals crop production, and would thus have serious social consequences. Many of the poorer villagers are gradually forced to abandon farming and to seek a livelihood elsewhere.

There have also been major changes in the pattern of livestock ownership. Most stock in the Sahel are now owned by village crop farmers, who have invested their surplus revenues from crop sales in livestock when crop prices were higher. They have also profited from low livestock prices during droughts to acquire more animals. Although providing manure and oxen for their fields, the animal's are principally maintained as a reserve of capital which can be called on in an emergency. As proof against inflation and as saleable assets, there is currently no other comparable investment. But the maintenance of such livestock contributes to the overstocking of pastures and to land degradation.

Pastures in the crop zone are increasingly utilized by village-based livestock to the detriment of transhumant herds which are steadily being squeezed out. This factor plus the declining area and productivity of pastures as the best land is brought under cultivation, increases the demand for crop residues for feed, which were previously available for transhumant herds but are now largely consumed by village-based stock. Many transhumant herds are moving south where crop residue output and pasture production are higher but the risk of trypanosomiasis is greater. But even here the scope for obtaining dry season feed is declining with the growth of population and village livestock. In the villages studied there has been a steady decline in the number of transhumant herds, and some transhumant livestock owners have settled and become mixed farmers producing their own crop residues. By settling in these villages they have established a claim to village pastures. In the long term transhumant production systems may be restricted to the low rainfall northern pastoral areas where crop farming is marginal.[48]

Wide variations in levels of income, wealth and household size were found in all villages. Cash incomes from crops were largely limited to groundnut and cotton producing farmers. Many farmers did not produce enough cereals to meet their domestic requirements. More and more emphasis is being given to income diversification, and all farmers in the villages studied in Senegal, Mali and Niger had some off-farm income sources, mostly remittances from migrant workers. Only cotton farmers in Burkina Faso were mainly dependent on crop revenues. A process of polarization of incomes was noted with richer farmers increasing their assets while poorer farmers were often obliged to sell assets during droughts, and eventually to abandon farming. The introduction of draft animals has also contributed to this polarization of incomes since it has permitted a substantial increase in cultivated areas.

Crop production and livestock raising in the Sahel are risky activities. In this "marginal" zone, farmers and pastoralists are forced to tackle the difficulties at three levels, (a) by adopting production strategies which reduce risks arising from climatic fluctuation and cope with the ecological marginality of the region; (b) by searching for income-generating activities (including migration) which enable producers to diversify and respond to economic constraints such as restricted levels of demand for agricultural products from the Sahel; and (c) by organizing themselves in village associations and producer groups in order to confront the political marginality which has characterized the inhabitants of this zone. Development policies in the region must take these key factors of marginalization into account.

Some Policy Recommendations

Considerable diversity in production systems both between households in a village and between villages was apparent. Among the villages studied in each country there were major variations in economic conditions due to resource, infrastructural, social, and political differences. For this reason, country comparisons are difficult, pointing to a need for more location-specific development planning. Regular surveying and monitoring work is now being carried out in the region to analyze farming systems and food security in the context of changing economic policies.[49]

Some aspects of further investigation into agricultural development problems in the Sahel were also explored, pinpointing the components of strategies which could be implemented to improve both farming systems and human welfare in this difficult environment. The main policy recommendations arising from the study are the following:

a. There is a desperate need to concentrate efforts on programs designed to allocate land rights to different groups of rural inhabitants, including both farmers and pastoralists, and to ensure their access to water and pasture resources. This will entail both the formulation of appropriate legislation, and the introduction of enhanced land-use management schemes.

b. The problem of declining soil fertility can be tackled through the vigorous promotion of efficient manure use and composting techniques (integration), as well as through the application of inorganic fertilizer where possible.

c. Improved fodder production schemes and intensive fattening of livestock can make an important contribution to increasing farmer's incomes, although there are numerous economic constraints, notably on the demand side, which must be overcome.

d. It would appear that further provision of draft animals and carts should only be undertaken after a careful assessment of the transport demand pattern in relation to existing supply, since there is a danger of saturating the market.

e. Extension and training programs in animal husbandry, which include specific attention to environmental issues, should be improved and targeted to both farmers and pastoralists.

f. Finally, a number of supplementary measures are important, including the development of credit and savings schemes, crop marketing and input supply arrangements, and the processing and distribution of animal products (including milk).

It is hoped that the results of this study will contribute to a greater understanding of the complexities of economic, social, and environmental change, and will encourage renewed efforts to assist in the development of indigenous integrated farming systems in the Sahel.

Annex 1 - Comments on the Methodology

To assist in the design of future studies of a similar nature, this annex outlines some of the strengths and weaknesses of the methodology adopted. During the various phases of field work and analysis, different approaches and issues were discussed at length and numerous problems identified. Some of the main difficulties were as follows.

In emphasizing the various ways in which farmers and households attempt to deal with the integration of crop production and livestock herding, attention focused on assessing the extent of socio-economic stratification. This led to the deliberate selection of both villages and households with different levels of assets, in particular ownership of draft animals. The household surveys included categories of households with and without draft animals, and livestock. But households who own these assets are over- represented. It was felt that because of the socio-economic stratification in the villages it was more useful to identify and describe the range of variation than look for the average. To this extent the approach was correct and the study has identified the wide variation in household assets and income, and has explained many of the factors underlying such variation.

It was not possible to relate the numbers of households sampled in different socio-economic categories to the whole village, since the sample of households was deliberately selective, based on ownership of assets. It is thus impossible to know what proportion of the total households in a village fall within the different categories. For the purposes of analyzing the diversity of production systems and the constraints to development it would also be useful to know the distribution of socio-economic categories within the villages. A random sample of village households would have provided a more accurate estimate of the extent of socio-economic stratification. This would have indicated the proportion of different socio-economic categories within villages. It would also have permitted a statistically acceptable use of average data for households. In one country (Senegal) a separate random sample of households in eight villages, including the six participating in the detailed household survey, was undertaken to overcome the weakness of selective sampling indicated above.[50]

Selective sampling was based on a number of factors the main one being the ownership of draft animals because their use in extending cultivation was a major concern of the study, and, being highly visible, their ownership is widely known in villages. Other criteria were ownership of livestock, both cattle and small ruminants, ethnic group, size of household and length of residence in the village. The use of these criteria as a basis for selective sampling has however, some major disadvantages.

Because land is becoming scarcer, it is the most valuable asset in the villages studied, and usufruct rights to land are the main factor determining subsequent ownership of other assets, household labor, livestock, draft animals, equipment, and so on. Second, although essential for expansion, the use of draft animals is not an essential condition for integration. Ideally the households should have been selected on the basis of permanent access to land, although it is recognized that obtaining information on individual land areas would have been difficult.

In the first phase there was problem in obtaining accurate information on key variables such as input levels, yields, labor use, and crop residue use.[51] This led to a greater emphasis on qualitative rather than quantitative data in the second phase. Anecdotal evidence and general impressions were taken into account, with the risk that in the absence of empirical data a subjective interpretation of the qualitative data could be influenced by preconceived ideas. However, to counteract such a risk, special efforts were made to consult appropriate literature and to compare the findings with other research results.

Where data could not be obtained in the villages, other sources were used which turned out to be less than satisfactory. The economic and agro-ecological conditions vary so much from village to village and from year to year that the reliability and relevance of data provided by parastatal institutions is very limited. Data from research institutions in all four countries were considered but were of limited value since few detailed production system surveys had been undertaken in or adjacent to the villages studied.[52]

On the issue of timing, the field work should have lasted at least one full year to monitor all inputs and outputs in the systems, and to follow all livestock management practices. However, after the first phase it was realized that it was almost impossible to establish a relationship of mutual confidence with the villagers in only three to five months, and that there was considerable reluctance among people questioned to provide information about livestock numbers and household expenditure for example. This, and other gaps in the data means that the conclusions and recommendations are based on information of varying quality.

Annex 2 - Details of the Areas Studied

The six villages which were studied in **Senegal** are situated in the Koungheul Arrondissement of the Sine Region. Four villages are situated to the north of the main east-west road linking Kaolack and Tambacounda and two to south of the road. They are all located in the area known as the groundnut basin.

The five villages which were studied in **Mali** are all located in the Cercle de Ségou in the Fourth Region. One village, Boussin, is situated to the east Ségou and the others are to the south and west. They are all south of the River Niger with one village, Somonodougouni, on its bank.

The five villages which were studied in **Burkina Faso** are located in Kossi Province, four of them in Kouka Département, and one, Kié, in Solenzo Département. They are all situated either on or close to the road which goes from Nouna through Solenzo to the main road from Bobo Dioulasso to Mali.

The six villages which were studied in **Niger** are located in Niamey Département and in Dosso Département. Four of the villages studied in the second phase are in Dosso Département, two in Gaya arrondissement, one in Dosso arrondissement, and one in Boboye arrondissement. The two retained from the first phase study are in Say arrondissement of Niamey Département.[53] Three of the villages are not far from the frontier with Nigeria, close to the main road from Dosso to Gaya.

Notes

1. There are various definitions of the Sahel region. According to standard agro-ecological and climatic classification, the Sahel (from the Arabic term meaning the "coast" of the Sahara desert) is a belt stretching across Africa from Senegal to Somalia, lying between the 200 mm and 400 mm rainfall isohyets (Kowal and Kassam, 1978). But, although the region is often considered as an isolated zone with its own special problems, "on ecological grounds as well as for historical and contemporary political and economic reasons, the Sahel should instead be seen as the northern part of a larger regional whole which includes the more humid Sudanian zone" (Gorse and Steeds, 1987, p.1). This is the definition used in this paper; and in this sense the region is often considered as co-terminus with the member states of CILSS (the Permanent Interstate Committee for Drought Control in the Sahel), comprising Burkina Faso, Cape Verde, Chad, the Gambia, Guinea Bissau, Mali, Mauritania, Niger and Senegal.

2. Many studies of crop and animal production systems in the Sahel have been carried out over the past two decades. Integration issues in the region have been explicitly treated in the reports and case studies by Benoit-Cattin (1986), Breman and others (1986a, 1986b and 1986c), Delgado (1978, 1979 and 1989), FAO (1983), Jahnke (1982), Landais and Lhoste (1990), Lhoste (1987), McIntire, Bourzat and Pingali (1988), Ruf (1985), Swift and others (1984), Swift (1985) and Toulmin (1983 and 1987). A bibliographic listing of some literature and reports used in this study is found in an annex to this paper.

3. A map of the study areas appears in Chapter 2.

4. Some of the methodological problems are summarized in Annex 1.

5. There is a good deal of controversy associated with the interpretation of evidence pertaining to climatic changes and trends in the region, as indicated in studies by, among others, Gorse and Steeds (1987), the IUCN (1989), and Rochette (1989, pp. 408-413).

6. Following standard terminology, the ethnic group known as the *Peul* in French have been called Fulani throughout this discussion, except where reference is made to a particular subgroup such as the *Peul Habobé.*

7. The papers by Bonnefond & Couty (1988) and by Commander, Ndoye and Ouédraogo (1989) present concise reviews of the changes in agricultural policy in Senegal during the 1980s, while Caswell (1984) summarizes the history of groundnut production and the parastatal, ONCAD.

8. Adjustment policies initiated in Mali at the beginning of the 1980s included measures to reduce the deficits incurred by parastatal crop marketing boards. The OACV was one of the parastatals which was closed down. This process, which has focused on the liberalization of cereals marketing, is described in various reports and studies including Staatz, Dioné and Dembélé (1989).

9. See the report by Fevrier and others (1986) for a survey of the livestock sector in Mali.

10. A comparison of agricultural production strategies in this and several other regions of Burkina Faso is found in the study by Thiombiano, Soulama and Wetta (1988).

11. An assessment of the difficulties faced by the CRPAs (extension services) in conjunction with agricultural policy reforms in Burkina Faso is given by Tallet (1989). See also Speirs (1991).

12. Agricultural policies in Niger during the 1980s are described and assessed in the report by Ancey and others (1988), which draws attention to the enormous problems of environmental degradation and the necessity of improving the management of natural resources. The study by Thebaud (1988) presents an examination of the livestock sector and the problems faced by pastoral communities notably in the eastern region of Niger.

13. The extent and the implications of cross border trade between Niger and Nigeria are described in recent work by Grégoire (1989), in connection with studies of regional markets and economic integration in West Africa.

14. Surveys of some of the techniques which are being used to protect and conserve the natural environment in the Sahel are presented in the study by Rochette (1989) which also includes an assessment of different "survival strategies." Further case studies, emphasizing the role of women in approaches to sustainable development in a number of Sahelian communities, are outlined by Monimart (1989).

15. The ramifications of structural adjustment programs in West Africa were initially explored in the papers edited by Guillaumont (1985), while details of the measures introduced in several Sahelian countries during the early and mid 1980s are surveyed by Martens (1987). The study by Lecaillon and Morrisson (1987) presents an analysis of economic performance and changing agricultural policies in low income countries including Burkina Faso and Mali.

16. Numerous studies have been carried out to explore the effects of structural adjustment programs on the agricultural sector in various African countries. Chhibber (1989) examines the effects of price changes on agricultural output through supply responses, while Lele (1989) and Weber and others (1988), assess the scope and limits of reforms in selected African countries including Senegal and Mali. Tinguiri (1990) describes the effects of economic policy changes on agriculture in Niger. There was no adjustment policy as such (based on loan agreements with the IMF and the World Bank) in Burkina Faso until early 1991.

17. Reardon and Matlon (1989) describe the factors which determine seasonal patterns of food insecurity in Burkina Faso, noting that "dependence on the market and thus vulnerability to market inefficiencies" are high, particularly in poor harvest years (p.134).

18. See also Figure 1. Cereals marketing issues in the Sahel, in relation to West African regional markets and international trade patterns, have been the subject of extensive analyses coordinated by the Club du Sahel/CILSS (1987 and 1989), and further surveyed by Bossard and Gabas (1989). The problem of competition with imports of wheat and rice is also assessed in these studies, and by Delgado (1991) and Reardon (1992). These food security and marketing issues are very complex, and cannot be treated in detail in this report; see, inter alia, the survey by Dioné (1990).

19. See the paper by Josserand (1989) for a discussion of changes in livestock production and meat markets in West Africa. Other studies of animal product marketing in Burkina Faso, Mali and Niger include: Arizo-Nino and others (1980), Delgado (1980) and USAID (1987). A concerted effort is now being made to improve marketing systems in the "central corridor" which links producers in Burkina Faso and Mali with the major markets in Cote d'Ivoire (Kulibaba and Holtzman, 1990).

20. On milk consumption and imports of dairy products in West Africa, see the paper by Seyoum (1989), summarizing the provisional results of research at ILCA. As Delgado (1991, p.109) observes: "It is striking that West Africa is virtually the only region of the world where cattle can live that does not have a viable local dairy industry. Even in Bamako, where notably progress has been made in this regard, 80 percent of milk consumed is imported, despite an estimated national dairy herd of roughly one milk cow per three inhabitants."

21. The "nexus" of interactions between population growth, agricultural production and environmental problems in Africa has been

explored in a recent study by Cleaver and Schreiber (1991).

22. See, among others, the study by Marty (1986) and the papers edited by Haubert and others (1985).

23. This season is known throughout the Sahel as *la soudure*, the hungry gap, during the rains and before the harvest when food supplies are at their lowest levels in the rural areas.

24. Reardon, Matlon and Delgado (1988) explore the different strategies adopted by households in a number of zones in Burkina Faso in order to cope with drought. The papers edited by Hill (1985) focus on the welfare of pastoralists and agro-pastoralists in the Niger Delta region of Mali. See also Corbett (1988), the classic study of entitlements and famine by Sen (1981), as well as the recent discussion of African famines by Watts (1991).

25. If de-mechanization is going to take place on a larger scale in the areas studied, this would add a new facet to an otherwise basically linear conceptualization of the mechanization process. See the study by Pingali, Bigot and Binswanger (1987).

26. Manure use in agro-pastoral production systems in the Sahel is also described in the case studies by Dicko and Sayers (1988), Powell and Mohamed-Saleem (1987), and Wilson (1986). It is important to note that the value of manure varies according to the source (from crop residues or from range grazing), and it varies in quality as fertilizer according to the ingested plant material.

27. See, among others, CILSS (1987), Dugué (1985), Penning de Vries and Djiteye (1982) and Sandford (1986).

28. There is an extensive literature describing and analyzing draft animal systems and the mechanization of crop production in Africa with case studies from the Sahel, including: Delgado and McIntire (1982), Fujioka (1987), Jahnke (1982), Munzinger (1982), Pingali, Bigot and Binswanger (1987) and Starkey (1987).

29. Table 4 estimates crop revenue in the villages studied.

30. Marie (1985) has investigated land tenure problems in connection with livestock production in the Niger Delta. The discussion of resource control and property rights in Africa by Berry (1984) is a useful background to this issue, and the study by Plateau (1988, pp.76-90) concludes that registration systems and the adjudication of land titles are important elements of strategies designed to reduce traditional inequalities and settle disputes over land access. See also Guyon (1989), Faye (1990) and Noronha (1985).

31. See the summary report on livestock activities (Club du Sahel/CILSS, 1988) and the atlas of pastoral production systems in the Sahel (CTA/IEMVT, 1989). Pastoral and rangeland production difficulties have been explored in several studies including the assessments of livestock development strategies in Burkina Faso, Mali and Niger by Breman and others (1986a, 1986b and 1986c), and by Benoit (1982a and 1984), Breman and De Wit (1983), Oxby (1975), Perrier (1986), Swift and Maliki (1984), Santoir (1983), and Van Keulen and Breman (1990).

32. In the meantime, conflicts between settled farmers and the groups of pastoralists and nomads in the northern Sahel are on the increase. Violent incidents arising through struggles over access to land and resources have been reported in many locations in recent years. These struggles inspired Brink, Bromley and Chavas (1991) to entitle their recent paper on agro-pastoral property rights in the Sahel, "the economics of Cain and Abel."

33. Gorse and Steeds (1987) estimated that the Sahelo-Sudanian zone of West Africa is capable of supporting a population of only 8.7 million on the basis of crop and livestock production, while the actual rural population numbered 11.1 million. This further underlines the difficulties of establishing sustainable production systems. However larger populations could be supported in the Sudanian and Sudano-Guinean zones to the south as indicated in table 4 (p.28) of their study. See also: Van Keulen and Breman (1990).

34. See, for example, the study of intensive sheep farming in Mali by Kolff and Wilson (1985).

35. Further evidence of the diversification into non-agricultural income-generating activities in Burkina Faso is presented by Reardon, Matlon and Delgado (1988).

36. The OECD (1988) study of the Sahel "facing the future" , (published in a revised version by Giri, 1989) outlines several different development scenarios for the Sahel which usefully complement this section. A trend scenario (in which economies stagnate and dependence on food imports and foreign aid increases) is compared with less favorable scenarios (where both drought and reduced foreign aid contribute to further social and economic decline and environmental degradation). This leads to consideration of possible "futures" based on economic reforms and changes in the roles of the "actors" including rural communities, governments and aid agencies.

37. The international commodity markets division of the World Bank does not project significant real price increases in groundnut oil or cotton until 1995 at the earliest.

38. On rural development and the popular participation issue see, among others, Chambers (1983) who argues for "bottom up" strategies ("putting the farmers first"), Gentil (1986) who explores the reasons for the failure of cooperative development schemes in West Africa, and Snrech (1988) who presents an analytic survey of the successes and failures of rural organizations in the Sahel.

39. Various examples of improved natural resource management, in the context of the "struggle against decertification" are given by Bonfils (1987), Kessler and Ohler (1983) and Rochette (1989). The *programme de gestion des terroirs* (land use management scheme) which has been initiated in Burkina Faso (CCCE, 1986) is particularly promising.

40. The title of this paper is owed in part to the remarkable study by Richards (1985) who makes a strong case for supporting an "indigenous agricultural revolution" in West Africa, building on "people's science" to experiment with often well known production techniques, rather than introducing research station results from the "top down."

41. As Van Keulen and Breman (1990) have argued, "the only real cure against 'land hunger' is increased productivity of the land, both in animal husbandry and in arable farming, requiring at least the import of phosphorus (fertilizer) from outside the system, because recycling of crop residues, manure and household waste, regeneration of degraded rangeland, anti-erosion measures, etc, may at best prevent further deterioration of the land resource, but are insufficient to lead to improvements" (p.194).

42. It should be noted that growing forage legumes as understory crops, or intercropping of legumes and cereals are possible strategies, and represent an important option under the declining fallow period constraint, since forage legumes accomplish soil restoration much faster than indigenous grasses (R. von Kaufmann, communication).

43. The important issue of improved animal health schemes in Africa has been explored in a recent paper by de Haan and Bekure (1991).

44. See, among others, the study by Adams and Vogel (1986).

45. As Reardon and Matlon (1989) noted, in policy terms, the seasonality of food insecurity in the Sahel underlines the need for "the maintenance of reserve stocks in close proximity to high-risk groups, through such approaches as village cereal banks" (p.136).

46. The paper by Lele and Christiansen (1989) presents a thorough assessment of marketing problems in the context of adjustment, based on a number of case studies, including Senegal and Nigeria in West Africa. Staatz, Dioné and Dembélé (1989) conclude their study of marketing reform in Mali by noting that: "If liberalization is to lead to improved market performance, it is not enough that the state stop doing certain things, like running monopoly marketing systems. The state must also take on new responsibilities, such as providing public information systems and improving credit markets, in order

to facilitate the private sector's ability to respond to its new opportunities" (p.715).

47. An assessment of fertilizer use and subsidies during the 1980s in selected African countries by Lele, Christiansen and Kadiresan (1989), concludes that there are strong arguments in favor of promoting the intensification of fertilizer use and of maintaining subsidies under specific conditions.

48. As Snrech (1990), and other observers have pointed out, there is a trend towards the emergence of two distinct animal production systems in West Africa: extensive, rangeland pastoral practices in the north; and more intensive, mixed farming further south.

49. See for example the reports published by the *projet diagnostic permanent* (CILSS, 1987a, 1987b, 1987c and 1990), as well as the research agenda outlined by Dioné (1990).

50. A separate paper has been published by Danida, presenting the results of the socio-economic analysis on which discussion in Chapter 3 is based. It is entitled: "Some Socio-economic Issues in the Development of Integrated Farming Systems in the Sahel".

51. The use of standard units of measurement is not widespread; in Niger, for example, farmers had no idea of field sizes.

52. The ISRA work in Senegal was an exception since they had carried out detailed surveys in a number of villages including one of those studied. ICRISAT and ILCA have also investigated integration issues as part of research programs in Mali and Niger.

53. Since this study was completed, an administrative reform in Niger has resulted in the absorption of Niamey Département within Tillabéri Département, and the creation of a new Communauté Urbaine de Niamey. The names of the arrondissements remain as before.

Bibliography

Adams, D. and R. Vogel (1986): Rural financial markets in low income countries - recent controversies and lessons. *World Development*, 14-4.

Ancey, G. and others (1988): Etude du secteur agricole du Niger - les politiques. Rapport de mission, Société d'Etudes pour le Développement Economique et Social, Paris.

Ariza-Nino, E. and others (1980): Synthesis - Upper Volta. In *Livestock and Meat Marketing in West Africa*, Vol I. Center for Research on Economic Development, University of Michigan.

Berry, S. (1984): The food crisis and agrarian change in Africa - a review essay. *African Studies Review*, 27-2.

Benoit, M. (1982a): *Nature peul du Yatenga - remarques sur le pastoralisme en pays* Mossi. ORSTOM, Paris.

Benoit, M. (1982b): *Les oiseaux de mil.* ORSTOM, Paris.

Benoit, M. (1984): *Le Seno Mango ne doit pas mourir - pastoralisme, vie sauvage et* protection au Sahel. ORSTOM, Paris.

Benoit-Cattin, M. (ed), (1986): Les unités expérimentales du Sénégal. ISRA/ CIRAD/FAC, Dakar, Montpellier, Paris.

Bonfils, M. (1987): *Halte à la désertification au Sahel.* Karthala, Paris.

Bonnefond, P. and P. Couty (1988): Sénégal - passé et avenir d'une crise agricole. *Revue Tiers Monde*, 114.

Bossard, L. and J-J. Gabas (1989): Agricultures Sahéliennes et marchés mondiaux - état de réflexions. D(89)324, Club du Sahel/CILSS, OCDE, Paris.

Breman, H. and C. De Wit (1983): Rangeland productivity and exploitation in the Sahel. *Science*, 221.

Breman, H. and others (1986a): Analyse de conditions de l'élevage et propositions de politiques et de programmes - Burkina Faso. (CABO, Wageningen) Club du Sahel/CILSS, OCDE, Paris.

Breman, H. and others (1986b): Analyse de conditions de l'élevage et propositions de politiques et de programmes - République du Niger. (CABO, Wageningen) Club du Sahel/CILSS, OCDE, Paris.

Breman, H. and others (1986c): Analyse de conditions de l'élevage et propositions de politiques et de programmes - République du Mali. (CABO, Wageningen) Club du Sahel/CILSS, OCDE, Paris.

Brink, R. van den, D. Bromley and J-P. Chavas (1991): The economics of Cain and Abel - agro-pastoral property rights in the Sahel. Cornell Food and Nutrition Policy Program, Working paper 11, CFNPP, New York.

Burkina Faso (1985): Politique de développement de l'élevage. Ministère de l'Agriculture et de l'Elevage, Ouagadougou.

Caswell, N. (1984): L'autopsie de l'ONCAD - la politique de l'arachide au Sénégal 1966-80. *Politique Africaine*, 14.

CCCE (1986): Rapport d'évaluation de la phase préparatoire d'un programme de gestion des terroirs villageois - Burkina Faso. Caisse Centrale de Coopération Economique, Paris.

Chambers, R. (1983): *Rural development - putting the last first.* Longman, Harlow.

Chhibber, A. (1989): The aggregate supply response - a survey. In Commander, S. (ed): *Structural adjustment and agriculture - theory and practice in*

Africa and Latin America. ODI/Currey/Heinemann, London.
CILSS (1987a): Burkina Faso - banque de données de base sur l'agriculture vivrière et l'élevage. CILSS - Projet Diagnostic Permanent, Ouagadougou.
CILSS (1987b): Mali - banque de données de base sur l'agriculture vivrière et l'élevage. CILSS - Projet Diagnostic Permanent, Ouagadougou.
CILSS (1987c): Sénégal - banque de données de base sur l'agriculture vivrière et l'élevage. CILSS - Projet Diagnostic Permanent, Ouagadougou.
CILSS (1987d): Projet développement des cultures fourragères et améliorantes en zone Soudano-Sahelienne - introduction, experimentations pratiques, régenération des sols et de la végétation, multiplication semencière, vulgarisation. CILSS/FAO, Ouagadougou.
CILSS (1990): Situation alimentaire - exercice 1989/90 et perspectives 1990/91. CILSS - Projet Diagnostic Permanent, Ouagadougou.
Cleaver, K. and G. Schreiber (1991): The population, agriculture and environment nexus in Sub-Saharan Africa. Draft paper - Africa Region, World Bank, Washington.
Club du Sahel and CILSS (1987): Cereals policies in Sahel countries - acts of the Mindelo conference. D(87)301, Club du Sahel/CILSS, OECD, Paris.
Club du Sahel and CILSS (1988): Livestock activities in the Sahel - Burkina Faso, Niger, Mali (the Sahelian livestock situation - restrictions, economic role and conditions for development). D(88)314, Club du Sahel/CILSS, OECD, Paris.
Club du Sahel and CILSS (1989): Regional cereals markets in West Africa - a compilation of studies on Sahelian agriculture, regional trade and world markets. Club du Sahel/CILSS, OECD, Paris.
Commander, S., O. Ndoye and I. Ouédraogo (1989): Structural adjustment and agriculture - Senegal 1979-88. In Commander, S. (ed): *Structural adjustment and agriculture - theory and practice in Africa and Latin America*. ODI/Currey/Heinemann, London.
Corbett, J. (1988): Famine and household coping strategies. *World Development*, 16-9.
CTA/IEMVT (1989): *Elevage et potentialités pastorales sahéliennes*. Centre Technique de Coopération Agricole et Rurale/Institut d'Elevage et de Médecine Vétérinaire des Pays Tropicaux, Wageningen and Paris.
de Haan, C. and S. Bekure (1991): Animal health in sub-Saharan Africa - initial experiences with alternative approaches. *World Bank Technical Paper*, 134.
Delgado, C. (1978): An investigation of the lack of mixed farming in the West African savanna - a farming systems approach for Tenkodogo, Upper Volta. Discussion paper 74, Center for Research on Economic Development, University of Michigan.
Delgado, C. (1979): Livestock versus foodgrain production in Southeast Upper Volta - a resource allocation analysis. In *Livestock Production and Marketing in the Entente States of West Africa, Vol I*. Center for Research on Economic Development, University of Michigan, Ann Arbor.
Delgado, C. (1980): Livestock and meat production, marketing and exports in Mali. In *Livestock and Meat Marketing in West Africa, Vol III*. Center for Research on Economic Development, University of Michigan.
Delgado, C. (1989): The changing concept of mixed farming in savanna West Africa - a conceptual framework applied to Burkina Faso. *Quarterly Journal of International Agriculture*, 28-3/4.
Delgado, C. (1991): Cereals protection and agricultural development strategy in the Sahel. *Food Policy*, April.
Delgado, C. and J. McIntire (1982): Constraints on oxen cultivation in the Sahel. *American Journal of Agricultural Economics*, 64-2.

Dicko, M. and R. Sayers (1988): Recherches sur le système agro-pastoral de production de la zone semi-aride du Niger - étude de la composante animale. Centre International pour l'Elevage en Afrique, Programme Niger, Niamey.

Dioné, J. (1990): Sécurité alimentaire au Sahel - point sur les études et projet d'agenda de recherche. Document de recherche 90-02, PRISAS, Institut du Sahel, Bamako.

Dugué, P. (1985): L'utilisation des résidus de récolte dans un système agro-pastoral Sahélo-Soudanien - le cas du Yatenga. *Cahiers de la Recherche-Développement*, 7.

Faye, J. (1990): Le control privé permet-il une meilleure gestion des ressources naturelles? Document présenté au séminaire "l'avenir de l'agriculture des pays du Sahel." Club du Sahel/CIRAD, Paris and Montpellier.

FAO (1983): Integrating crops and livestock in West Africa. *Animal Production and* Health Paper, 41.

Février, M. and others (1986): Mali - rapport de la mission de revue du secteur élevage. FAO, Rome.

Fujioka, K. (1987) Draft animal power - 25 years of experience in French speaking Africa. *World Animal Review*, 63.

Gentil, D. (1986): *Les mouvements coopératifs en Afrique de l'Ouest - interventions de l'Etat ou organisations paysannes?* L'Harmattan, Paris.

Gersovitz, M. and J. Waterbury (eds), (1987): *The political economy of risk and choice in Senegal*. Frank Cass, London.

Giri, J. (1989): *Le Sahel au XXIe siècle - un essai de réflexion, prospective sur les* sociétés sahéliennes. Karthala, Paris.

Gorse, J. and D. Steeds (1987): Desertification in the Sahelian and Sudanian zones of West Africa. *World Bank Technical Paper*, 61.

Grégoire, E. (1989): Etat et réseaux marchands dans le commerce des vivres au Niger. Document présenté au séminaire: Les espaces céréaliers régionaux en Afrique de l'Ouest, Club du Sahel/ CILSS, Lomé.

Guillaumont, P. (ed), (1985): *Croissance et ajustement - les problèmes de l'Afrique de l'Ouest*. Economica, Paris.

Guyon, G. (1989): Faut-il se préoccuper des questions foncières - jusqu'où et comment? *Notes et Etudes*, 21, CCCE, Paris.

Haubert, M., C. Frelin, and N. Trong nam Tran (ed), (1985): *Politiques alimentaires* et structures sociales en Afrique Noire. PUF, Paris.

Hill, A. (ed), (1985): *Population, health and nutrition in the Sahel - issues in the welfare of selected West African communities*. KPI, London.

IUCN (1989): *The IUCN Sahel studies*. International Union for the Conservation of Nature and Natural Resources, Gland.

Jahnke, H. (1982): *Livestock production systems and livestock development in tropical Africa*. Kieler Wissenschaftsverlag, Kiel.

Josserand, H. (1989): Effets des importations de viandes extra-Africaines sur les échanges de bovins entre les pays d'Afrique de l'Ouest. Document présenté au séminaire: Les espaces céréaliers régionaux en Afrique de l'Ouest, Club du Sahel/CILSS, Lomé.

Kessler, J. and F. Ohler (1983): Interventions dans les pays du Sahel - une approche écologique. Centre de Recherches Agrobiologiques, Wageningen.

Kolff, H. and R. Wilson (1985): Livestock production in central Mali - the "mouton de case" system of smallholder sheep fattening. *Agricultural Systems*, 16.

Kowal, J. and A. Kassam (1978): *Agricultural ecology of the savanna - a study of West Africa*. OUP, Oxford.

Kulibaba, N. and J. Holtzman (1990): Livestock marketing and trade in the Mali/Burkina Faso - Cote d'Ivoire corridor. Abt Associates/USAID, Washington.

Landais, E. and Ph. Lhoste (1990): L'association agriculture-élevage en Afrique intertropicale - un mythe techniciste confronté aux réalités du terrain. *Cahier des Sciences Humaines*, 26-1/2.

Lecaillon, J. and others (1987): *Economic policies and agricultural performance of low* income countries. Development Centre Studies, OECD, Paris.

Lele, U. (1989): Managing agricultural development in Africa - lessons of experience for governments and aid donors. *Finance and Development*, 26-1.

Lele, U. and R. Christiansen (1989): Markets, marketing boards and cooperatives in Africa - issues in adjustment policy. MADIA working paper, World Bank, Washington.

Lele, U., R. Christiansen and K. Kadiresan (1989): Issues in fertiliser policy in Africa - lessons from development programs and adjustment lending 1970-87. MADIA working paper, World Bank, Washington.

Lhoste, Ph. (1987): L'association agriculture-élevage - évolution du système agro-pastoral au Sine-Saloum. Etudes et Synthèses de l'IEMVT, 21. Institut d'Elevage et de Médecine Vétérinaire des Pays Tropicaux, Paris.

Marie, J. (1985): Elevage et problèmes fonciers dans le delta intérieur du Niger au Mali. *Cahiers de la Recherche-Développement*, 7.

Martens, A. (1987): L'ajustement structurel en vitesse de croisière au Sahel? D(87)312, Club du Sahel/CILSS, OCDE, Paris.

Marty, A. (1986): Une approche de la classification sociale en milieu rural sahélien. Brochure 50, AMIRA, Paris.

Matlon, P. (1987): Potential and practice in food production technology development - the West African semi-arid tropics. In Mellor, J., C. Delgado and M. Blackie (ed): *Accelerating food production in sub-Saharan Africa*. Johns Hopkins, Baltimore.

McIntire, J., D. Bourzat and P. Pingali (1988): Crop livestock interactions in sub - Saharan Africa - technologies and research priorities. Working paper, International Livestock Centre for Africa, Addis Ababa.

Monimart, M. (1989): *Femmes du Sahel - la désertification au quotidien*. Karthala, Paris.

Munzinger, P. (1982): *Animal traction in Africa*. Gesellschaft für Technische Zusammenarbeit, Eschborn.

Noronha, R. (1985): A review of the literature on land tenure systems in Sub-Saharan Africa. Report 43, Research Unit of the Agriculture and Rural Development Department, World Bank, Washington.

OECD (1988): *The Sahel facing the future - increasing dependence or structural* transformation. OECD, Paris.

Orsini, J., P. Lhoste, A. Boucher, A. Faye and L. Niang (1985): Une typologie d'exploitations agropastorales au Sine-Saloum, Sénégal. *Revue d'Elevage et de Médecine Vétérinaire des Pays Tropicaux*, 38-2.

Oxby, C. (1975): *Pastoral nomads and development*. International Africa Institute, London.

Perrier, G. (1986): Limiting livestock pressure on public rangeland in Niger. Pastoral Network Paper 21d, Overseas Development Institute, London.

Penning de Vries, F. and A. Djitèye (ed), (1982): La productivité des pâturages sahéliens - une étude des sols, des végétations et de l'exploitation de cette ressource naturelle. Agricultural Research Report 918, PUDOC, Wageningen.

Pingali, P., Y. Bigot and H. Binswanger (1987): *Agricultural mechanisation and the* evolution of farming systems in Sub-Saharan Africa. Johns Hopkins University Press/World Bank, Baltimore and Washington.

Platteau, J-P. (1988): The food crisis in Africa - a comparative structural analysis. Working paper 44, World Institute for Development Economics Research, Helsinki.

Powell, J. and M. Mohamed-Saleem (1987): Nitrogen and phosphorus transfers in a crop-livestock system in West Africa. *Agricultural Systems*, 25.

Reardon, T. (1992): Cereals demand in the Sahel and potential impacts of regional cereals protection. *World Development*, forthcoming.

Reardon, T., P. Matlon and C. Delgado (1988): Coping with household level food insecurity in drought-affected areas of Burkina Faso. *World Development*, 16-9.

Reardon, T. and P. Matlon (1989): Seasonal food insecurity and vulnerability in drought-affected regions of Burkina Faso. In Sahn, D. (ed): *Seasonal variability in third world agriculture - the consequences for food security.* Johns Hopkins, Baltimore.

République du Mali (1987a): Revue du secteur agricole du Mali. Ministère de l'Agriculture, Bamako.

République du Mali (1987b): Mémento - intégration agriculture-élevage. Ministère de l'Agriculture/Compagnie Malienne pour le Développement des Textiles, Bamako.

République du Niger (1986): Schéma d'aménagement agricole. Ministère de l'Agriculture, Niamey.

République du Niger (1988): Politique d'exportation du bétail du Niger. Rapport du Projet Elevage Intégré. Ministère des Ressources Animales et de l'Hydralique/USAID, Niamey.

République du Sénégal (1986): Etude du secteur agricole - rapport de synthèse. Ministère du Développement Rural, Dakar.

Richards, P. (1983): Ecological change and the politics of African land use. *African* Studies Review, 26-2.

Richards, P. (1985): *Indigenous agricultural revolution.* Hutchinson, London.

Rochette, R. (ed), (1989): *Le Sahel en lutte contre la désertification* - leçons d'experiences. CILSS/GTZ, Ouagadougou and Eschborn.

Ruf, T. (1985): Pour une intégration de l'élevage bovin dans les périmètres irrigués de l'Office du Niger au Mali. *Cahiers de la Recherche-Développement*, 7.

Ruthenberg, H. (1980): *Farming systems in the tropics.* (third edition) OUP, Oxford.

Sandford, S. (1983): *The management of pastoral development in the third world.* Wiley, New York.

Sandford, S. (1986): Crop residue-livestock relationships. Unpublished working paper, International Livestock Centre for Africa, Addis Ababa.

Santoir, C. (1983): *Raison pastorale et développement - les problèmes des peuls* sénégalais face aux aménagements dans la vallée du Sénégal. ORSTOM, Paris.

Sautier, D., M. O'Deye and N. Bricas (1989): *Mil, maïs, sorgho - techniques et* alimentation au Sahel. PUSAF/ L'Harmattan, Paris.

SEDES (1975): *Recueil statistique de la production animale.* Société d'Etudes pour le Développement Economique et Social, Paris.

Sen, A. (1981): *Poverty and famine - an essay on entitlement and deprivation.* OUP, Oxford.

Seyoum, S. (1989): Consumption of dairy products in West Africa - past trends and future prospects. African Livestock Policy Analysis Network, paper 23, International Livestock Centre for Africa, Addis Ababa.

Snrech, S. (1988): La dynamique d'organisation du monde rural Sahélien. D(88)325, Club du Sahel/ CILSS, OCDE, Paris.

Snrech, S. (1990): Les années 1980 dans le Sahel - bilan et perspectives pour l'agriculture et le monde rural. D(90)358, Club du Sahel/CILSS, OCDE, Paris.

Speirs, M. (1991): Agrarian change and the revolution in Burkina Faso. *African Affairs*, 90-358.

Staatz, J., J. Dioné and N. Dembélé (1989): Cereals market liberalisation in Mali. *World Development*, 17-5.

Starkey, P. (1987): Animal traction - brief donkey work. *Ceres*, 120.

Swift, J. and others (1984): Pastoral development in central Niger - report of the Niger range and livestock project. USAID, Niamey.

Swift, J. (ed), (1985): Pastoral and agropastoral production systems in central Mali - three case studies. International

Livestock Centre for Africa, Addis Ababa.

Swift, J. and A. Maliki (1984): Cooperative development experiments among nomadic herders in Niger. Pastoral Development Network Paper 18c, Overseas Development Institute, London.

Tallet, B. (1989): Le CNR face au monde rural - le discours à l'épreuve des faits. *Politique Africaine*, 33.

Thebaud, B. (1988): *Elevage et développement au Niger*. ILO, Geneva.

Thiombiano, T., S. Soulama and C. Wetta (1988): *Les systèmes alimentaires au Burkina Faso*. CEDRES, Serie des Résultats de Recherche 001, Université de Ouagadougou.

Tinguiri, K. (1990): Crise économique et ajustement structurel, 1982-88 (au Niger). *Politique Africaine*, 38.

Toulmin, C. (1983): Herders and farmers or farmer-herders and herder-farmers? Pastoral Network Paper 15d, Overseas Development Institute, London.

Toulmin, C. (1986): Changing patterns of investment in a Sahelian community. Unpublished thesis.

Toulmin, C. (1987): Drought and the farming sector - loss of farm animals and post-drought rehabilitation. In: Menyonga, J., T. Bezuneh and A. Youdeowei (eds): *Food grain production in semi-arid Africa*. SAFGRAD, Ouagadougou.

USAID (1988): Study of constraints to increased exports of agropastoral products in Niger. Development Alternatives Inc/USAID, Niamey.

Van Keulen, H. and H. Breman (1990): Agricultural development in the West African Sahelian region - a cure against land hunger? *Agriculture, Ecosystems and Environment*, 32.

Watts, M. (1991): Entitlements or empowerment? Famine and starvation in Africa. *Review of African Political Economy*, 51.

Weber, M. et al (1988): Informing food security decisions in Africa - empirical analysis and policy dialogue. *American Journal of Agricultural Economics*, 70-5.

Wilson, R. (1986): Central Mali - cattle husbandry in the agropastoral system. *World Animal Review*, 58.

World Bank (1989a): *Sub-Saharan Africa - from crisis to sustainable growth.* World Bank, Washington.

World Bank (1989b): *World Development Report, 1989*. World Bank, Washington.

Distributors of World Bank Publications

ARGENTINA
Carlos Hirsch, SRL
Galeria Guemes
Florida 165, 4th Floor-Ofc. 453/465
1333 Buenos Aires

AUSTRALIA, PAPUA NEW GUINEA, FIJI, SOLOMON ISLANDS, VANUATU, AND WESTERN SAMOA
D.A. Books & Journals
648 Whitehorse Road
Mitcham 3132
Victoria

AUSTRIA
Gerold and Co.
Graben 31
A-1011 Wien

BANGLADESH
Micro Industries Development Assistance Society (MIDAS)
House 5, Road 16
Dhanmondi R/Area
Dhaka 1209

Branch offices:
156, Nur Ahmed Sarak
Chittagong 4000

76, K.D.A. Avenue
Kulna 9100

BELGIUM
Jean De Lannoy
Av. du Roi 202
1060 Brussels

CANADA
Le Diffuseur
C.P. 85, 1501B rue Ampère
Boucherville, Québec
J4B 5E6

CHINA
China Financial & Economic Publishing House
8, Da Fo Si Dong Jie
Beijing

COLOMBIA
Infoenlace Ltda.
Apartado Aereo 34270
Bogota D.E.

COTE D'IVOIRE
Centre d'Edition et de Diffusion Africaines (CEDA)
04 B.P. 541
Abidjan 04 Plateau

CYPRUS
Cyprus College Bookstore
6, Diogenes Street, Engomi
P.O. Box 2006
Nicosia

DENMARK
SamfundsLitteratur
Rosenoerns Allé 11
DK-1970 Frederiksberg C

DOMINICAN REPUBLIC
Editora Taller, C. por A.
Restauración e Isabel la Católica 309
Apartado de Correos 2190 Z-1
Santo Domingo

EGYPT, ARAB REPUBLIC OF
Al Ahram
Al Galaa Street
Cairo

The Middle East Observer
41, Sherif Street
Cairo

EL SALVADOR
Fusades
Alam Dr. Manuel Enrique Araujo #3530
Edificio SISA, ler. Piso
San Salvador 011

FINLAND
Akateeminen Kirjakauppa
P.O. Box 128
SF-00101 Helsinki 10

FRANCE
World Bank Publications
66, avenue d'Iéna
75116 Paris

GERMANY
UNO-Verlag
Poppelsdorfer Allee 55
D-5300 Bonn 1

GUATEMALA
Librerias Piedra Santa
5a. Calle 7-55
Zona 1
Guatemala City

HONG KONG, MACAO
Asia 2000 Ltd.
46-48 Wyndham Street
Winning Centre
2nd Floor
Central Hong Kong

INDIA
Allied Publishers Private Ltd.
751 Mount Road
Madras - 600 002

Branch offices:
15 J.N. Heredia Marg
Ballard Estate
Bombay - 400 038

13/14 Asaf Ali Road
New Delhi - 110 002

17 Chittaranjan Avenue
Calcutta - 700 072

Jayadeva Hostel Building
5th Main Road Gandhinagar
Bangalore - 560 009

3-5-1129 Kachiguda Cross Road
Hyderabad - 500 027

Prarthana Flats, 2nd Floor
Near Thakore Baug, Navrangpura
Ahmedabad - 380 009

Patiala House
16-A Ashok Marg
Lucknow - 226 001

Central Bazaar Road
60 Bajaj Nagar
Nagpur 440010

INDONESIA
Pt. Indira Limited
Jl. Sam Ratulangi 37
P.O. Box 181
Jakarta Pusat

ISRAEL
Yozmot Literature Ltd.
P.O. Box 56055
Tel Aviv 61560
Israel

ITALY
Licosa Commissionaria Sansoni SPA
Via Duca Di Calabria, 1/1
Casella Postale 552
50125 Firenze

JAPAN
Eastern Book Service
Hongo 3-Chome, Bunkyo-ku 113
Tokyo

KENYA
Africa Book Service (E.A.) Ltd.
Quaran House, Mfangano Street
P.O. Box 45245
Nairobi

KOREA, REPUBLIC OF
Pan Korea Book Corporation
P.O. Box 101, Kwangwhamun
Seoul

MALAYSIA
University of Malaya Cooperative Bookshop, Limited
P.O. Box 1127, Jalan Pantai Baru
59700 Kuala Lumpur

MEXICO
INFOTEC
Apartado Postal 22-860
14060 Tlalpan, Mexico D.F.

NETHERLANDS
De Lindeboom/InOr-Publikaties
P.O. Box 202
7480 AE Haaksbergen

NEW ZEALAND
EBSCO NZ Ltd.
Private Mail Bag 99914
New Market
Auckland

NIGERIA
University Press Limited
Three Crowns Building Jericho
Private Mail Bag 5095
Ibadan

NORWAY
Narvesen Information Center
Book Department
P.O. Box 6125 Etterstad
N-0602 Oslo 6

PAKISTAN
Mirza Book Agency
65, Shahrah-e-Quaid-e-Azam
P.O. Box No. 729
Lahore 54000

PERU
Editorial Desarrollo SA
Apartado 3824
Lima 1

PHILIPPINES
International Book Center
Fifth Floor, Filipinas Life Building
Ayala Avenue, Makati
Metro Manila

POLAND
ORPAN
Palac Kultury i Nauki
00-901 Warzawa

PORTUGAL
Livraria Portugal
Rua Do Carmo 70-74
1200 Lisbon

SAUDI ARABIA, QATAR
Jarir Book Store
P.O. Box 3196
Riyadh 11471

SINGAPORE, TAIWAN, MYANMAR,BRUNEI
Information Publications Private, Ltd.
02-06 1st Fl., Pei-Fu Industrial Bldg.
24 New Industrial Road
Singapore 1953

SOUTH AFRICA, BOTSWANA
For single titles:
Oxford University Press Southern Africa
P.O. Box 1141
Cape Town 8000

For subscription orders:
International Subscription Service
P.O. Box 41095
Craighall
Johannesburg 2024

SPAIN
Mundi-Prensa Libros, S.A.
Castello 37
28001 Madrid

Librería Internacional AEDOS
Consell de Cent, 391
08009 Barcelona

SRI LANKA AND THE MALDIVES
Lake House Bookshop
P.O. Box 244
100, Sir Chittampalam A. Gardiner Mawatha
Colombo 2

SWEDEN
For single titles:
Fritzes Fackboksforetaget
Regeringsgatan 12, Box 16356
S-103 27 Stockholm

For subscription orders:
Wennergren-Williams AB
Box 30004
S-104 25 Stockholm

SWITZERLAND
For single titles:
Librairie Payot
1, rue de Bourg
CH 1002 Lausanne

For subscription orders:
Librairie Payot
Service des Abonnements
Case postale 3312
CH 1002 Lausanne

TANZANIA
Oxford University Press
P.O. Box 5299
Maktaba Road
Dar es Salaam

THAILAND
Central Department Store
306 Silom Road
Bangkok

TRINIDAD & TOBAGO, ANTIGUA BARBUDA, BARBADOS, DOMINICA, GRENADA, GUYANA, JAMAICA, MONTSERRAT, ST. KITTS & NEVIS, ST. LUCIA, ST. VINCENT & GRENADINES
Systematics Studies Unit
#9 Watts Street
Curepe
Trinidad, West Indies

UNITED KINGDOM
Microinfo Ltd.
P.O. Box 3
Alton, Hampshire GU34 2PG
England

VENEZUELA
Libreria del Este
Aptdo. 60.337
Caracas 1060-A

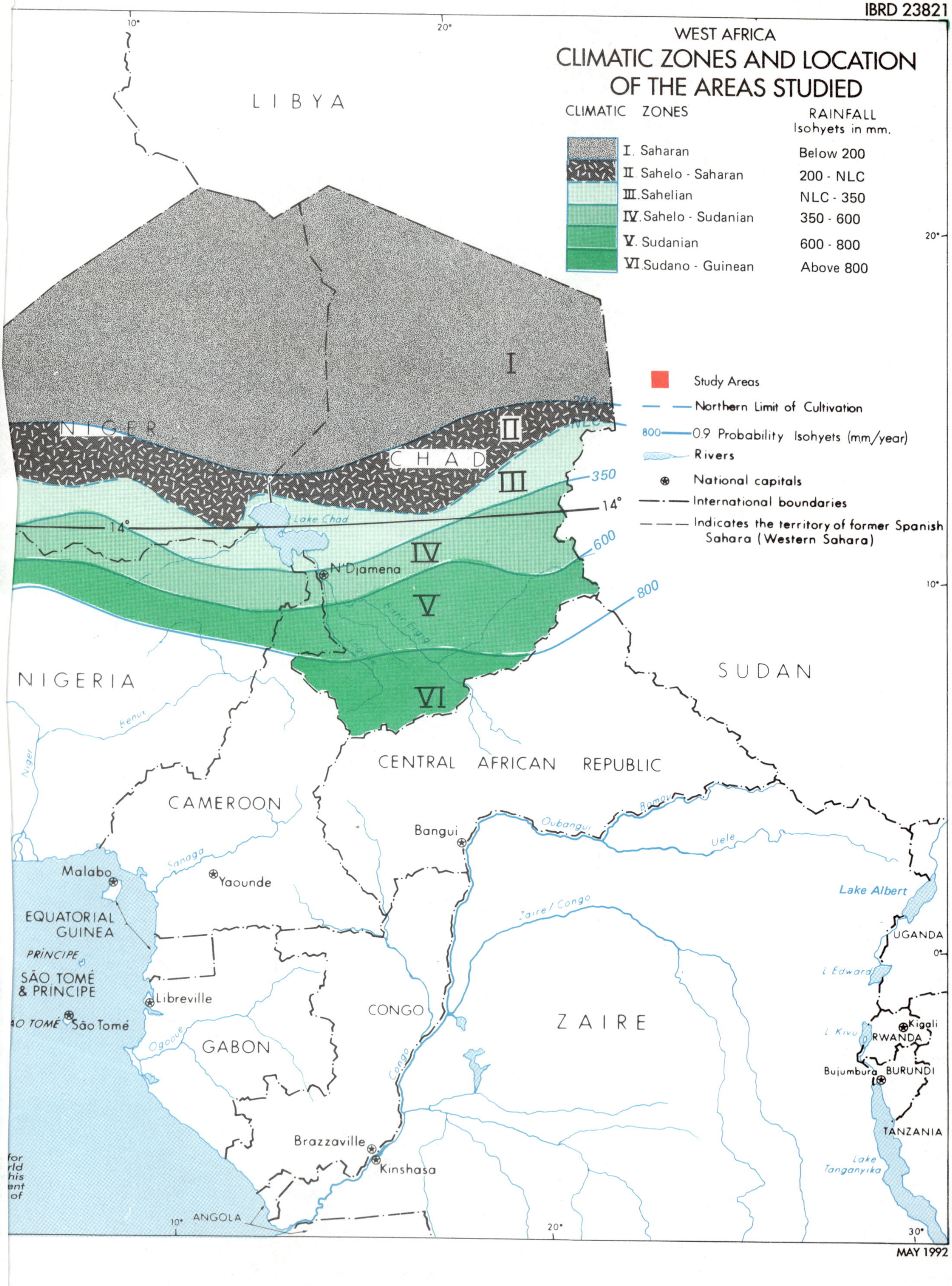
IBRD 23821
WEST AFRICA
CLIMATIC ZONES AND LOCATION OF THE AREAS STUDIED
CLIMATIC ZONES
RAINFALL Isohyets in mm.
I. Saharan
Below 200
II. Sahelo - Saharan
200 - NLC
III. Sahelian
NLC - 350
IV. Sahelo - Sudanian
350 - 600
V. Sudanian
600 - 800
VI. Sudano - Guinean
Above 800
Study Areas
Northern Limit of Cultivation
800 0.9 Probability Isohyets (mm/year)
Rivers
National capitals
International boundaries
Indicates the territory of former Spanish Sahara (Western Sahara)
LIBYA
NIGER
CHAD
NIGERIA
SUDAN
CENTRAL AFRICAN REPUBLIC
CAMEROON
EQUATORIAL GUINEA
PRINCIPE
SÃO TOMÉ & PRINCIPE
GABON
CONGO
ZAIRE
UGANDA
RWANDA
BURUNDI
TANZANIA
ANGOLA
Lake Chad
N'Djamena
Bahr Erguig
Logone
Benue
Niger
Bangui
Oubangui
Bomou
Uele
Malabo
Yaounde
Sanaga
Libreville
São Tomé
Ogooue
Zaire/Congo
Congo
Brazzaville
Kinshasa
Lake Albert
L. Edward
L. Kivu
Kigali
Bujumbura
Lake Tanganyika
350
600
800
14°
10°
20°
30°
0°
MAY 1992

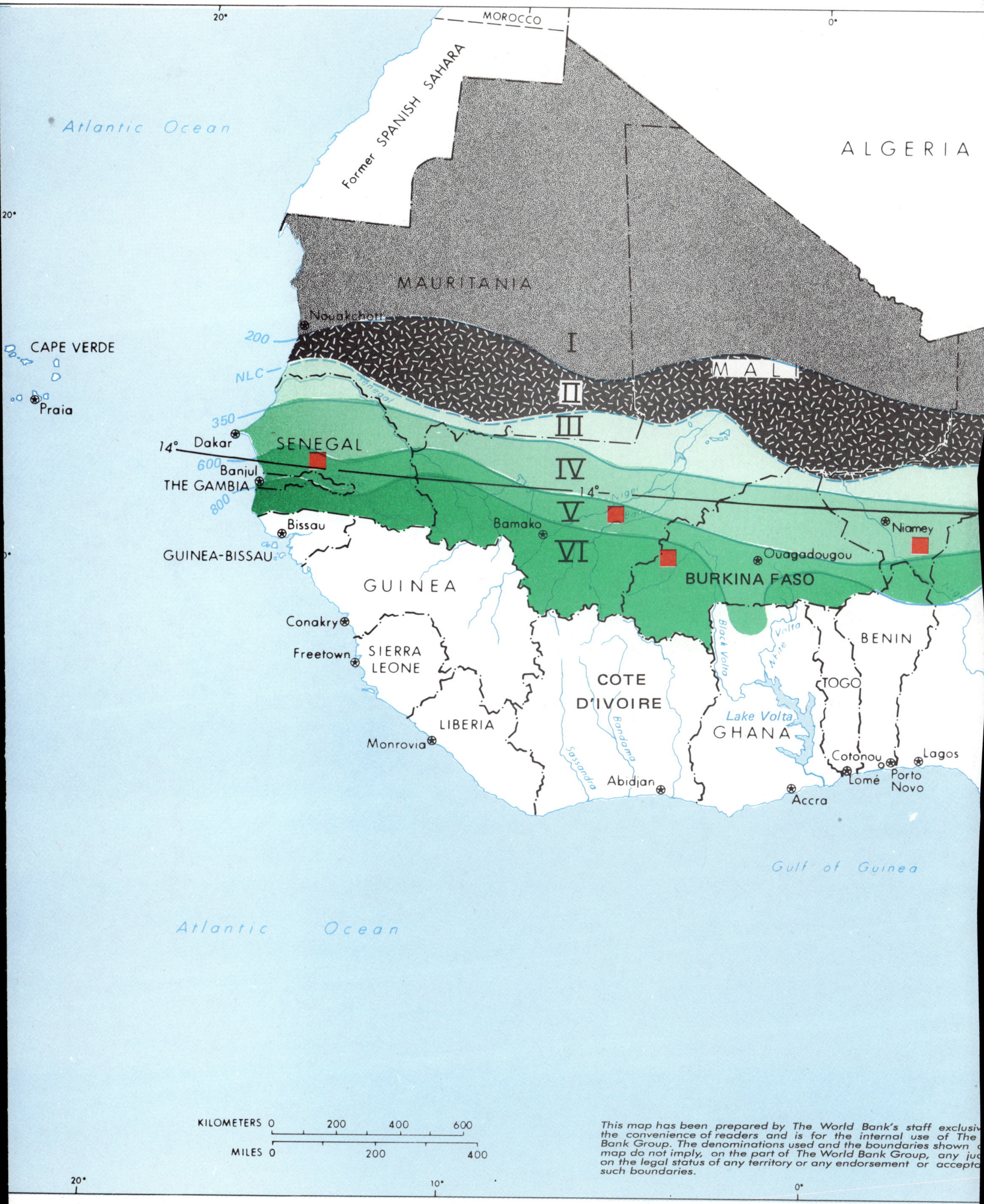
MOROCCO
Former SPANISH SAHARA
ALGERIA
Atlantic Ocean
MAURITANIA
Nouakchott
CAPE VERDE
Praia
200
NLC
350
600
800
I
II
III
IV
V
VI
MALI
SENEGAL
Dakar
Banjul
THE GAMBIA
14°
Bissau
GUINEA-BISSAU
Bamako
Niger
Niamey
Ouagadougou
BURKINA FASO
GUINEA
Conakry
Freetown
SIERRA LEONE
LIBERIA
Monrovia
COTE D'IVOIRE
Sassandra
Bandama
Abidjan
Black Volta
White Volta
Volta
Lake Volta
GHANA
Accra
TOGO
Lomé
BENIN
Cotonou
Porto Novo
Lagos
Gulf of Guinea
Atlantic Ocean
KILOMETERS 0 200 400 600
MILES 0 200 400
20°
10°
0°
This map has been prepared by The World Bank's staff exclusiv the convenience of readers and is for the internal use of The Bank Group. The denominations used and the boundaries shown o map do not imply, on the part of The World Bank Group, any ju on the legal status of any territory or any endorsement or accepta such boundaries.